OSPREY COMBAT AIRCRAFT • 14

HALIFAX SQUADRONS
OF WORLD WAR 2

OSPREY
AVIATION

SERIES EDITOR: TONY HOLMES

OSPREY COMBAT AIRCRAFT • 14

HALIFAX SQUADRONS
OF WORLD WAR 2

Jon Lake

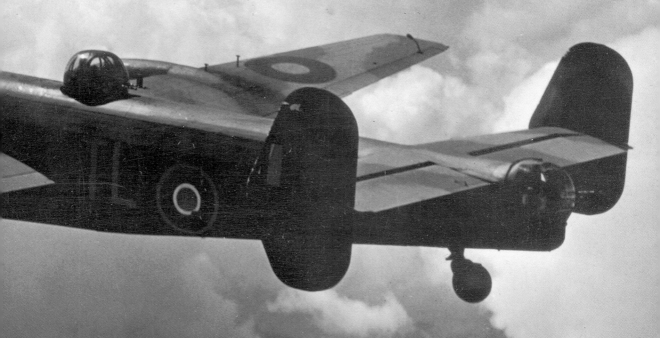

Front cover
Flt Lt Ron Hines, RAAF, was the captain of No 462 Sqn's 'N-Nan' (MZ913), one of the *Airborne Cigar*-equipped Halifax B IIIs assigned to the unit – *Airborne Cigar* (ABC) was a powerful jammer which disrupted German fighter control frequencies. Adorned with suitable 'girlie' nose art and the name *Jane*, 'N-Nan' flew her last sortie on 10 April 1945, participating in a 'spoof' raid against Berlin to draw enemy fighters away from the night's Main Force target, which was the southern city of Leipzig. No 100 Group's spoof raids became progressively more realistic, with target marker flares being dropped and aircraft transmitting on No 8 Group Master Bomber frequencies. 'N-Nan' developed engine trouble on the way back from the target and limped home into a stiff headwind to Manston.

A truly superb heavy bomber, the Hercules-engined Halifax was even superior to the Lancaster, boasting better multi-role versatility and a lower loss rate by war's end. The aircraft was particularly prized by No 100 Group, who appreciated the type's comfortable and capacious fuselage. Indeed, by VE-Day the programme of standardisation onto the Halifax by specialist units within the group was well advanced (*Cover artwork by Ian Wyllie*)

Title page spread
This No 35 Sqn Halifax B II Series I was written off during a raid on Nuremberg on 28/29 August 1942, by which time the unit was operating as part of the Pathfinder Force. The Merlin-engined Halifax was Bomber Command's best, and most effective, bomber until the introduction of the higher-flying and faster Lancaster (*via Phil Jarrett*)

For a catalogue of all titles published by Osprey Military, Aviation or Automotive please write to:
The Marketing Manager,
Osprey Publishing Limited,
P.O. Box 140, Wellingborough,
Northants NN8 4ZA,
United Kingdom

Or visit our website:
www. ospreypublishing.com

First published in Great Britain in 1999 by Osprey Publishing
Elms Court, Chapel Way, Botley, Oxford, OX2 9LP

ISBN 1 85532 892 5

Edited by Tony Holmes
Page design by TT Designs, T & B Truscott
Cover Artwork by Iain Wyllie
Aircraft Profiles by Chris Davey
Figure Artwork by Mike Chappell
Scale Drawings by Mark Styling

Origination by Valhaven Ltd, Isleworth, UK
Printed through Bookbuilders, Hong Kong

00 01 02 03   10 9 8 7 6 5 4 3 2

EDITOR'S NOTE
To make this best-selling series as authoritative as possible, the editor would be extremely interested in hearing from any individual who may have relevant photographs, documentation or first-hand experiences relating to the elite pilots, and their aircraft, of the various theatres of war. Any material used will be fully credited to its original source. Please write to Tony Holmes at 10 Prospect Road, Sevenoaks, Kent, TN13 3UA, Great Britain.

CONTENTS

INTRODUCTION

Almost anyone with an interest in aviation would think that they knew the 'broad-brush' story of Bomber Command, and of its main aircraft types. Driven by the relentless energy of the obsessive Arthur 'Bomber' Harris, the Command concentrated on the area bombing of German cities by night, with the primary aims of destroying industrial centres and sapping the morale of the civilian population and industrial workforce. The USAAF, by contrast, surgically attacked precision targets by day.

Within Bomber Command, the useless Avro Manchester was transformed by powerplant change into the Lancaster, which arrived relatively late, but which was thereafter the most effective bomber, carrying heavier loads, more bomb types and enjoying superior performance and better crew survivability than its poor relations. Handley Page's Halifax was very much second best – a great improvement over the Short Stirling and Vickers Wellington, but no match for the Lancaster.

That, at least, is the conventional wisdom.

The Halifax served only with Bomber Command's 'junior' Bomber Groups, No 4 in Yorkshire, and later the Canadian-manned No 6 Group (and later still, albeit briefly and in tiny numbers, with the Pathfinders). The other groups (based in East Anglia) enjoyed a higher profile, and in 1939 had been equipped with more modern aircraft – Battles, Blenheims, Wellingtons and Hampdens, rather than No 4 Group's ageing Whitleys.

And during the early years of the war, the new Stirlings and Manchesters went to Nos 3 and 5 Groups, whilst No 4 Group had to wait for the Halifax. But even the group's brief period operating the Command's most modern bomber was destined to be a short one, with the other groups soon 'leap-frogging' to the more glamorous Lancaster.

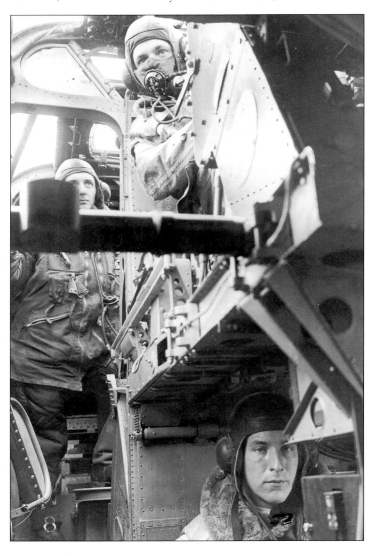

Early flying kit reveals the age of this photograph, which features the crew of an early in-service B I or B II. Shown here are the flight engineer (standing), the pilot (in oxygen mask) and the wireless operator. The navigator sat at his chart table in front of the wireless operator, and three or four gunners were also carried (*via* Aeroplane)

Another view of the Halifax cockpit, showing the pilot's main panel and the massive throttle quadrant, with its power and pitch levers. The bucket-like shape of the pilot's seat was intended to allow the pilot to wear a seat-type parachute (*via* Aeroplane)

Such was the publicity attached to the new Avro aircraft, that it was sometimes derisively referred to as the '*Daily Mirror* bomber' by Halifax aircrew, who were understandably irked by the newer design's 'headline-hogging'.

As was so often the case, Bomber Command's commander was blunt, highly critical and controversial when it came to the Halifax;

'I will state categorically that one Lancaster is to be preferred to four Halifaxes. Halifaxes are an embarrassment now, and will be useless for the bomber offensive in six months, if not before. The Halifax suffers about four times the casualties for a given bomb tonnage when compared to the Lancaster. Low ceiling and short range make it an embarrassment when planning attacks with Lancasters.'

Air Vice Marshal Don Bennett, a former Halifax pilot and the AOC of No 8 Group, was only marginally less scathing, saying that the aircraft was 'not as good as the Lancaster, but nevertheless did a sound job of work'.

It is a fact that the Halifax could not carry the bombload of the Lancaster, nor could it range quite so far. The Halifax also had a marginally lower ceiling, although it was never low enough for the aircraft to receive the mauling meted out to aircraft like the Stirling from hostile flak. The Halifax was incapable of carrying the very largest weapons, but the aircraft was very much better than its critics gave it credit for. Even the early Merlin-engined versions were not markedly inferior than the Lancaster, and were an enormous improvement over the Stirling or Wellington, while the later Hercules-engined Halifaxes were superior in some respects to the famed Avro bomber.

Taken overall, the Halifax suffered a loss rate of one in every 21.05 sorties, while the Lancaster loss rate was one per 27.2 sorties, but either

9

Sitting on a fold-away seat beside the pilot on take-off and landing, the flight engineer had his own panel behind the pilot's seat, allowing him to control the engines and fine-tune fuel flow and power (*via* Aeroplane)

figure marked a remarkable improvement over the Stirling, which suffered one loss for every 10.7 sorties. The Lancaster's lower loss rate also partly reflected the aircraft's dominance during the later stages of the war, flying what almost became 'milk runs', and by its absence during the most difficult and costly year of the bomber war, 1941. Equally, the Halifax rate was distorted by the very heavy losses suffered in 1941 and early 1942 – before the Lancaster was even in frontline service.

It is perhaps worth emphasising that in No 8 Group service, from August 1942, the Halifax suffered a loss rate of only 2.5 per cent, while the Lancaster suffered 3.7 per cent, the Stirling 5.4 per cent and the Wellington 6 per cent. In the type of daylight raids which predominated at the end of the war, the Halifax also came out ahead, with a loss rate of 0.56 per cent compared to the Lancaster's 0.74 per cent. All available evidence would suggest that the Hercules-engined Halifax enjoyed a lower loss rate than the supposedly superior Lancaster.

And while over the whole span of the war the average Lancaster crew statistically lasted for about six sorties more than the average Halifax crew, once they were shot down, they were very much less likely to survive. Twenty-nine per cent of Halifax aircrew shot down survived the experience, compared to 17 per cent of Stirling aircrew and only 11 per cent of Lancaster aircrew. The Halifax had a larger, more capacious, fuselage than the Lancaster, in which movement was easier, and from which bailing out was less difficult. But human casualties were never an over-riding priority to 'Bomber' Harris, and aircrew alive in enemy *Stalags* and *Offlags* were of little use to him. All that counted to Harris were bombs on target. The fact was that in its typical 21.05 sortie lifetime, an 'average' Halifax would deliver only 100 tons of bombs, while the 'average' Lancaster crew delivered 154 tons in their 27.2 sorties.

There was also some thought at the time that a typical Halifax crew were more likely to put their ordnance on target due to the fact that they bombed from a slightly lower altitude in rather greater comfort than the aircrew in the higher-flying, but more cramped, Lancasters. But percentage points of accuracy were arguably of little interest to Harris, who focused on destroying area targets, not in saturating only the aim point.

The Halifax was also a better multi-role aeroplane, proving more adaptable to maritime, meteorological reconnaissance, para-dropping, glider-towing, ECM, Elint and out-of-area operations. Perversely, this may even have counted against the Halifax in the eyes of 'Bomber' Harris, who remained steadfast and implacable in his opposition to 'diverting' four-engined 'heavies' to do anything other than raze German cities, and especially Berlin. But Harris was not alone in his hostility to the aircraft. The strengths of the Halifax were not generally recognised, and indeed the aircraft's contribution to the war effort was often ignored.

As a typical example of this, take the raid on Saarbrücken on the

night of 13 January 1945. Bomber Command reportedly sortied 'a force of 234 Lancasters and Mosquitoes'. In fact, on that night the fleet had consisted of 20 Lancasters, 12 Mosquitoes and a staggering 201 Halifaxes, which had somehow escaped the attention of the Bomber Command officers who wrote the press release! It has similarly been widely forgotten that the Halifax made a bigger contribution to Bomber Command's war effort than any other aircraft, apart from the Lancaster, dropping more bombs (224,207 tons in 36,995 sorties) than the Battle, Blenheim, Boston, Fortress, Hampden, Manchester, Mitchell, Mosquito, Stirling, Ventura and Wellington combined. This should not come as any big surprise, for at its peak, the Halifax force comprised 35 squadrons, equipped with 1500 aircraft.

Finally, while the Halifax was almost certainly slower and lower-flying than the Lancaster, with a smaller bombload, more crucially it was more expensive to build. Some believed that the resources dedicated to its production would have been better devoted to the Lancaster. In short, though no-one would have used the phrase at the time, it was widely believed that the Lancaster gave 'more bang for your buck'. And as if this

The Boulton Paul E type turret was fitted in the tail position of most Halifaxes. This turret boasted four 0.303-in Browning machine guns, as shown here in this ground-mounted training turret (*via* Aeroplane)

Late-model Halifaxes (some B VIs and A IXs) used a Boulton Paul D type turret, fitted with a pair of Browning 0.50-in heavy machine guns. These packed a considerable punch, and gave the Halifax a more worthwhile 'sting in the tail' (*via* Aeroplane)

were not reason enough for the Avro bomber's pre-eminence, in an air force in which all decision makers and 'movers and shakers' were ex-pilots, the Lancaster was arguably a better pilot's aeroplane (at least in its original form).

This led to the general consensus verdict that the Halifax was 'second best' at the time, and this verdict has naturally been accepted since. But it should be remembered that reputations can be set in stone early-on, and may then be difficult to revise. Certainly the Halifax is widely remembered as being a lesser aircraft, although closer examination of all the facts may lead the

Armourers make ready to load 500-lb bombs aboard a Halifax. Unlike the Lancaster, Halifaxes lacked the ability to carry Bomber Command's largest weapons (*via* Aeroplane)

Women workers put the finishing touches to an anonymous Halifax B II. Many of these aircraft were produced from sub-assemblies by the London Passenger Transport Board, which formed the London Aircraft Transport Group (*via* Phil Jarrett)

impartial observer to challenge history's verdict.

And just as the Halifax won a largely undeserved reputation, in retrospect it would seem that the popular view of Bomber Command is also based largely on misconception. This popular view is that Bomber Command's night bombing campaign was little more than terror-bombing, attacking area targets (German cities) with woeful inaccuracy, while the USAAF, by day, conducted precision bombing of pinpoint targets. This is a gross over-simplification.

Bomber Command's reputation would seem to be based more on its performance early in the war, before the establishment of the Path Finder Force (PFF), and before the widespread use of sophisticated navigation and bombing aids like *Gee*, *Oboe* and H2S. Bombing for 'moral' (psychological) effect was stressed by the RAF's first commander, Lord Trenchard, who had previously commanded the Independent Force of semi-strategic bombers in World War 1, and who embraced the concept of 'moral' effect (he admitted to using the term because he had difficulty spelling the word psychological) partly because the material effect of early bombing raids was so puny!

However, between the wars, the RAF became wedded to the idea that the best use of airpower was to crack the morale of the enemy population before he could break the morale of ours! It was widely assumed that lumbering bombers would best be employed by night, when they would be less vulnerable to enemy fighters, or to visually directed anti-aircraft guns. America, by contrast, had played no real part in the bombing offensive in World War 1, and was able to examine the results of the RFC and RAF's bombing more clinically. It concluded that the best way forward was to attack key industries much more selectively. This in turn led the USAAC to look at high altitude performance and defensive firepower as the best ways of ensuring that bombers reached their targets, and at daylight raids as being the way to ensure accuracy.

In the earliest days of World War 2, Bomber Command was limited to attacking 'military' targets in an effort to avoid escalation. However, German attacks on cities, and the ineffectiveness of early British efforts, led to the Bombing Directive of St Valentine's Day 1942, which urged a switch to attacks on German

A No 35 Sqn B II in flight at low level over the English countryside during May 1942. this unit was the first RAF squadron to bomb Berlin, with pilot, Flt Lt Leonard Cheshire, gaining a measure of fame during the years that followed. The unit also participated in attacks on the *Tirpitz* in Trondheim Fjord, and in the historic 1000 Bomber Raid against Köln at the end of May 1942 (*via* Aeroplane)

cities, with the declared aim of undermining the morale and 'breaking the spirit' of the enemy civilian populace, and especially its factory workers.

When America finally joined the war, it tenaciously stuck to the strategy of daylight precision bombing. The B-17 was ill-suited to anything else, national pride and independence were at stake, and years of indoctrination were hard to shake – even as it became clear that daylight bombing in gin-clear conditions over Nevada or Arizona were a very different proposition to attempting the same thing in a European winter, in skies swarming with enemy fighters. Throughout the war, weather ensured that only about 50 per cent of bombs dropped by the Eighth Air Force were dropped visually, and in non-visual bombing, the Americans had an appalling record of inaccuracy. They were simply never as good as the RAF at radar-directed 'blind bombing'. The USAAF didn't do 'blind bombing', and never trained its radar operators as thoroughly as did the RAF. As if that were not serious enough, individual bombing runs soon gave way to pattern bombing, with a whole 'combat box' bombing on the leader's command. Accuracy suffered as a result.

Heavy losses and poor weather soon forced a switch in USAAF bombing strategy, although this was never admitted. More and more, attacks were directed against targets described as railway marshalling yards – often a convenient euphemism for an area attack against an entire city! By contrast, Bomber Command continued to attack cities, but the introduction of the PFF, target marking and H2S increased accuracy until a nominally 'area' attack against a city would devastate its industrial area and railway yards, but would cause less destruction elsewhere!

In the latter part of the war, RAF Bomber Command was actually more successful at placing its bombs on target than was the Eighth Air Force. When Albert Speer compared USAAF daylight attacks and RAF night attacks against the oil industry, he concluded that;

'The RAF night attacks are considerably more effective than the US daylight attacks, since heavier bombs are used, and an extraordinary accuracy in attacking the target is reported.'

Thus, although there continued to be a considerable difference between the British and American bomber offensives in theory, in practise not much separated them.

But while capable of great accuracy and precision, Bomber Command was seldom given pinpoint targets, and certainly AOC-in-C Bomber Command was never happy with what he saw as diversionary operations, opposing pinpoint attacks against various targets, and even objecting to the diversion of resources to create the PFF – whose primary role was only to improve the accuracy of Main Force bomber operations. So, perhaps the precision versus terror bombing debate is of little more than academic interest. Like so many legends, the Bomber Command inaccuracy myth thus has some foundation in truth, but falls very far short of telling the true story.

Halifax B IIIs swarm over the French coast near Calais during the long tactical bombing campaign which preceded D-Day. The Halifax proved enormously popular with its crews, although it was dismissed by others as being 'second best' to the Lancaster (*via Phil Jarrett*)

The ruggedness, reliability and survivability of the Hercules-powered Halifax B III was demonstrated by the fact that no less than four of these aircraft exceeded 100 operational sorties. *FRIDAY THE 13th* clocked up a remarkable 128 sorties (*via* Aeroplane)

ORIGINS OF THE HALIFAX

Since World War 1, Handley Page Ltd had been the traditional suppliers of heavy bombers for the Royal Air Force, from the O/400 (the so-called 'Bloody Paralyser') and the huge V/1500 to the Hyderabad, Hinaidi and Heyford. The company's dominance was only challenged by Vickers with the Vimy and Virginia. The company was slow to embrace the monoplane configuration, however, and the Heyford (which entered service in 1933) was relatively short-lived, replaced by Armstrong Whitworth Whitleys and Vickers Wellesleys. These monoplanes were both considerably faster and longer ranged than the anachronistic Heyford, and promised to be less vulnerable to enemy fighters.

Although Handley Page won major production orders for its Hampden medium bomber, it was Short Brothers which received the contract to develop the first truly modern heavy bomber, which became the Stirling. At virtually the same time, the Air Staff issued a new specification for an equally advanced medium bomber to be powered by a pair of Rolls-Royce Vulture engines. This specification resulted in the Avro Type 679 (later the Manchester) and the Handley Page HP.56, which eventually became the Halifax.

Two HP.56 prototypes, each to be powered by twin Vulture engines, were ordered on 30 April 1937. At the last moment, however, it became clear that Vulture production would be inadequate to meet the needs of the Avro 679 and the HP.56, and it was decided that the HP.56 would be redesigned with four Merlin engines as the HP.57. The name 'Halifax' was agreed, but kept secret. The biggest change was to the wing, whose span was increased from 88 ft to 98 ft 8 in – four inches short of the maximum allowable width, which had been dictated by the dimensions of the largest hangars then available to the RAF.

First prototype HP.57 Halifax L7244 is seen at Boscombe Down in May 1945, powered by Merlin X engines. The aircraft was never fitted with armament, but did gain leading edge slats (*Author's collection*)

When the decision was taken to make the Halifax a four-engined aircraft, Handley Page strongly favoured using radials, considering powerplants such as the Bristol Taurus, the Wright Cyclone and the Pratt & Whitney Twin Wasp, as well as the in-line Napier Dagger. Handley Page also suggested using Hercules HE-65Ms with 100-octane fuel, but the Air Ministry instead chose the less-powerful combination of the HE-15M running on 87-octane as the basis for comparison with the Merlin. This showed the Merlin Halifax to have a longer range (but lower speed), and the prototypes therefore received four 1145 hp Merlin X engines.

Handley Page was no more successful in gaining its choice of defensive armament than it had been with its choice of engines. The company wanted to use Frazer-Nash turrets in mid-upper and 'mid-under' positions, but was instead forced to use a Boulton Paul tail turret, augmented by a nose turret and two floor-mounted machine guns.

The first prototype (hand-built at Cricklewood) was unarmed, and completed its first flight (at RAF Bicester) on 25 October 1939. It had de Havilland two-position variable-pitch propellers with metal blades. Despite secrecy and tight security, the airfield's perimeter was thronged

The second Halifax prototype was the first fitted with armament, as shown here. L7245 was briefly used by the Halifax Conversion Flight, before being employed as a ground instructional airframe. The distinctive bomb bays in the inner wings can just be discerned in this unusual view of the aircraft (*via Phil Jarrett*)

Senior Handley Page personnel pose in front of an early Halifax B II, powered by Merlin XX engines. When it entered service, the Halifax was the most modern bomber the RAF had ever seen, although not the largest, as it was smaller all-around than the Short Stirling (*via Aeroplane*)

This early Halifax B II was extensively used for trials. It is seen here in typical early bomber configuration, with aerial masts and beam gun hatches. It subsequently became the B II prototype (*Author's collection*)

The same aircraft is seen later in its career, with extended inboard engine nacelles and a modified, streamlined nose (*Author's collection*)

with cars and onlookers, amongst whom was almost certainly the German air attaché!

The armed second prototype flew on 17 August 1940, and was fitted with Rotol constant-speed propellers with Schwarz wooden blades. Consideration was later given to re-engining the production Halifax with Griffon or Sabre engines, and to fitting 0.50-in machine guns in the turrets, but in fact the initial production B I differed very little from the prototypes. The production aircraft had the same Merlin X engines, but with Rotol constant-speed airscrews with magnesium blades. An initial batch of 100 was ordered on 7 January 1938, almost two years before the prototype had made its maiden flight.

HALIFAX GOES TO WAR

Bomber Command was, for much of the war, Britain's only way of carrying the war to the enemy. Powerless to intervene in Poland, British Army units were soon ejected from Scandinavia and France. Apart from commando raids, and fighting in peripheral 'side-shows' like North Africa, the British Army then had little opportunity to engage the enemy until D-Day. Britain's powerful fleet was hard-worked protecting convoys from U-boats, and imposing a blockade on Germany, but had little more to do against an enemy which was not a maritime power. Only by bombing targets in Germany could Britain 'fight back'.

But despite this, Bomber Command made a tenuous start to the war, being initially prohibited from attacking targets other than German warships and naval ports with anything more deadly than propaganda leaflets! The Command began the war singularly ill-equipped for a real strategic bombing campaign, relying primarily on twin-engined, short-ranged aircraft like the Wellington, Hampden and the near-obsolete Whitley, and on the Fairey Battle and Bristol Blenheim (see *Osprey Combat Aircraft 5 – Blenheim Squadrons of World War 2* for further details) for tactical bombing. None of these aircraft were designed for night and all-weather flying, boasting few creature comforts for their crews.

And the first of the Command's 'modern heavies' was little better. The Stirling was underpowered and under-armed, and proved to be not only ferociously vulnerable but also incapable of hitting the enemy hard. It was the Stirling which prompted one Luftwaffe fighter general to observe that he was 'entirely satisfied' that Britain was building four-engined bombers, for they were just as easy to shoot down as a medium bomber, and cost the British more in men and more to build.

Entering service soon after the Stirling, the twin-Vulture engined

This B II Series I wears the 'ZA-' codes of No 10 Sqn, which converted to the Halifax in December 1941 at Leeming. Like many of the squadron's early aircraft, it has a low demarcation between the upper surface disruptive camouflage and the black undersides (*via Phil Jarrett*)

No 76 Sqn, which re-formed at Linton-on-Ouse in May 1941, was the RAF's second Halifax unit, following No 35 Sqn, whose C Flight formed its cadre. This well-known aircraft was flown by Christopher Cheshire, brother of Leonard (*via Bruce Robertson*)

Another view of the 'other' Cheshire's Halifax. The aircraft has a wavy demarcation between its black undersides and the camouflaged topsides, a common, if non-standard, feature at this stage of the war. It was lost on a 52-aircraft raid on Magdeburg on 15/16 August 1941, being the only one of the nine Halifaxes destroyed on that operation to be shot down by a nightfighter. Cheshire became a Prisoner of War (*via Phil Jarrett*)

Manchester was undeniably modern in concept, but was fatally flawed by its powerplants, which failed with depressing regularity. The Manchester reached Bomber Command in November 1940, and began flying operations in late February 1941. The third aircraft in the trio of new types to enter squadron ranks in late 1940 was the Halifax, which also suffered some teething problems – especially with its hydraulic system and undercarriage – but was soon to demonstrate that it had far greater potential than either the Manchester or Stirling.

The first unit within the RAF to receive the Handley Page 'heavy' was No 35 Sqn, which was resurrected at Boscombe Down on Bonfire Night, 1940. The squadron collected its first Halifax on 13 November, and moved to No 4 Group, and RAF Leeming, on 20 November. The unit borrowed the prototype, L7244, from the Ministry of Aircraft Production for crew conversion and training, and then moved again on 5 December to Linton-on-Ouse, which was another No 4 Group station.

The squadron flew its first operational mission on the night of 11/12 March, despatching seven aircraft to bomb Le Havre. At that time Bomber Command was heavily engaged in anti-shipping operations from Cherbourg to Wilhelmshaven, and the campaign later intensified between July and November 1941 after hesitant beginnings. Each aircraft carried 12 500-lb bombs, and planned to attack from 13,000 ft. One aborted, and cloud forced another to bomb Dieppe – the secondary target – whilst a third jettisoned its bombload. Four aircraft bombed the primary target, but one of these was later downed by a friendly fighter on its way home, with only the pilot and flight engineer managing to bail out.

No 76 Sqn became the second Halifax unit to form, again at Linton (under Wg Cdr Bufton), on 1 May 1941, and commenced flying operations on 12 June, having by then moved to Middleton St George. The day before, nine No 35 Sqn Halifaxes had been among 80 aircraft sortied to

bomb Duisberg (although, in reality, the force actually attacked Köln).

No 76 Sqn's first operation was also the RAF's first 'all four-engined' raid of the war, with three of the unit's Halifaxes joining eight from No 35 Sqn and seven Stirlings – the target was a rubber plant at Hüls, and Sgt Godwin's crew claimed a Bf 109 shot down during the course of the mission. On 20 June the tables were turned, though, and a Bf 110 claimed the first Halifax lost to enemy action. On 30 June six No 35 Sqn aircraft participated in a daylight attack on Kiel, the mission's prime purpose being to test the concept of daylight raids by heavy bombers. One Halifax was downed, but two Bf 110s were in turn claimed destroyed.

July saw a general return to targeting German industry, although without stopping the campaign against naval targets and ports. A Bomber Command report had concluded that;

'The successful attack of a specific target at night can only be made under clear moonlight. Therefore, for three-quarters of each month it is only possible to obtain satisfactory results by heavy, concentrated attacks on large working class and industrial areas in carefully selected towns.'

The Command's initial priority target list focused on industrial towns which were also railway centres, including Duisberg, Düsseldorf, Hamm, Köln, Osnabruck, Schwerte and Soest, with Bremen, Frankfurt, Hamburg, Hannover, Mannheim and Stuttgart as secondaries.

This change in strategy by Bomber Command did not suddenly mean

Yet another variation in camouflage is displayed by this No 35 Sqn Halifax B II, with a high and fairly regularly scalloped demarcation line. No 35 Sqn had been the RAF's first Halifax unit, initially equipped with the original B I (via Phil Jarrett)

The early Merlin-engined Halifaxes never looked as graceful as the Lancaster, and the heavily framed bomb-aimer's glazing and bulbous nose turret looked 'draggy', while the small, triangular, tailfins similarly never looked quite right. But the Halifax B I and B II performed sterling service, and were all Bomber Command had in the way of modern bombers for a vital year of the war (via Phil Jarrett)

No 35 Sqn must have selected this aircraft for a photo sortie because of its pristine finish, since it looks 'nearly new', apart from some exhaust staining on the tops of the wings. Wearing completely standard camouflage and markings, this aircraft typified the bulk of Halifax B IIs delivered to Bomber Command (*via Phil Jarrett*)

The Halifaxes of No 78 Sqn 'joined the fight' on the night of 29/30 April 1942 during an attack on Ostend. The squadron traded Whitleys for Halifaxes at Croft in March 1942, soon moving to Middleton St George (*via Phil Jarrett*)

that naval targets were ignored, and the next high profile raid undertaken by Halifaxes was against the pocket battleship *Scharnhorst* in La Rochelle harbour on 24 July. Fifteen aircraft from Nos 35 and 76 Sqns went in unescorted, and five were lost to a force of 18 Bf 109s. Only one hit was claimed, although five were actually scored, and five fighters claimed. *Scharnhorst* limped back to Brest, having shipped 3000 tonnes of water.

One of No 35 Sqn's earliest crews was that of the then Flg Off Geoffrey Leonard 'Skip' Cheshire, who was later to become arguably Bomber Command's most distinguished pilot. Cheshire, and his crew – Sgts Brown, Gutteridge (observer), Hares, Jackson, Roberts and Weldon – were credited as being the first RAF bomber crew to attack Berlin, in July 1941. In September that year, Cheshire flew 1700 miles to attack Turin, thus setting another Bomber Command record.

Cheshire had trained with Oxford University Air Squadron and then flew a tour on Whitleys, before joining No 35 Sqn, with whom he won a DFC and successive promotions to flight lieutenant and squadron leader, and with whom he flew on the first 1000 Bomber Raid to Cologne. Cheshire was one of the rare breed of aircrew who felt no fear and no apprehension, and this won him a reputation for ice coolness under stress.

He began his third tour of operations in August 1942 as the new CO of another Halifax unit, No 76 Sqn. Cheshire was unique in winning a Victoria Cross (VC) whose citation made it clear that the award was for his cold and calculated acceptance of risks, and for 'leading from the front' over an extended period, and not for an individual act of heroism. While not a 'Halifax VC' in the truest sense, Cheshire flew two of his four operational tours on Halifaxes, with one each on Whitleys and Lancasters.

Returning to 1941, in August of that year the publication of the Butt report underlined the inaccuracy and ineffectiveness of the bombing campaign. This study, by D M Butt, a member of the Cabinet secretariat, had been commissioned by Prime Minister Winston Churchill's Chief Scientific Adviser. 'The average crew, in average weather, couldn't find their way to the target', was how Harris paraphrased the report's conclusions. Confidence in the Command was further undermined when Churchill compared its efforts to the Charge of the Light Brigade.

Such criticism forced a move away from selective targeting on 'vital cogs', and further emphasised the need to heavily attack area targets. The decision was therefore taken to conserve aircraft and crews until there were sufficient to inflict real damage. Halifaxes were not involved in the operation to Berlin on 7/8 November, but the effect of the alarming 12.4 per cent loss rate encountered during the sortie was felt throughout the Command. Air Chief Marshal Sir Richard Peirse was discredited, and it became clear that there would soon be major changes.

The capaciousness of the Halifax fuselage can be seen in this photo of a No 78 Sqn B II. From a similar angle, the Lancaster would look significantly more 'skinny'. It was this deep fuselage which later allowed the Halifax to be so successfully adapted as an EW platform and for Airborne Forces and SOE work (*via Brice Robertson*)

Halifax B V V9985 was used to test re-contoured bomb bay doors, which allowed the Halifax to carry the big 4000-lb and 8000-lb bombs. The bulged doors were not adopted, and in-service Halifaxes carried the bigger bombs with their doors 'ajar' (*via Dr Alfred Price*)

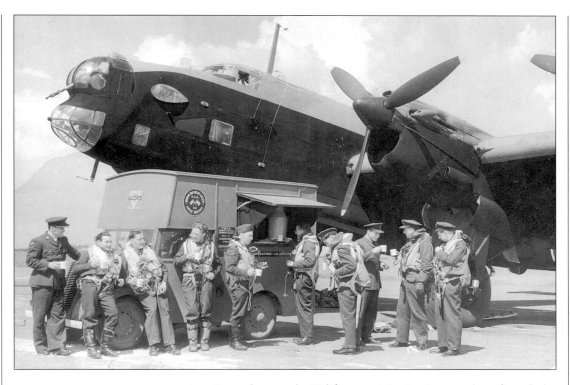

An American-funded 'tea van' brings refreshment to the crew of this RCAF Halifax. Although belonging to a Canadian squadron, few of the aircrew wear the distinctive 'Canada' shoulder flash. At this early stage of the war, five of the eight crew are commissioned, and only the NCOs are wearing flying boots! (*via Aeroplane*)

Nose-art was relatively uncommon in Bomber Command until quite late in the war, and No 405 Sqn's 'R-Robert' (W7710), nicknamed the *'RUHR VALLEY EXPRESS'*, was a noteworthy exception. The wartime caption tells us that 'after each raid, another truck is added' (*via Aeroplane*)

December saw the Halifaxes participating in a number of attacks by day and by night on German capital ships 'holed up' in the port of Brest. By this time the squadrons were equipped with improved B IIs, most of which were fitted with a C II mid-upper gun turret. A third Halifax unit, No 10 Sqn, had by then formed at Leeming, and began joining the offensive. Operation *Veracity I* on 18 December again explored the practicality of day bombing, and involved six Halifaxes from No 35 Sqn, six from No 76 and five from No 10, together with Stirlings, Manchesters and fighter cover. Operation *Veracity II* on 30 December involved only Halifax bombers (with a Spitfire escort), but these ran into very heavy defences and three aircraft (and two crews) were lost.

Attacks against the *Kreigsmarine* also continued with an abortive attempt by nine Halifaxes to mine *Tirpitz* in the Aas Fjord – thick cloud prevented the aircraft (flying from Lossiemouth) from finding their target. Brest's importance as a target ended with the 12 February 1942 'Channel Dash' by the German battleships *Scharnhorst*, *Gneisenau* and the battlecruiser *Prinz Eugen*. Halifaxes were involved in the efforts to halt their flight, but poor weather meant that only one of the big bombers was able to drop its stick of bombs, and the German vessels made good their escape.

Arthur 'Bomber' Harris (known to his friends as 'Butch') took over as AOC-in-C Bomber Command in February 1942. Harris was the former Deputy Chief of the Air Staff, and had also commanded No 5 Group. His Command comprised just 378 aircraft, including 69 'heavies', and his immediate priority was to expand its strength and effectiveness. Under Harris, Bomber Command gained a new priority target list, including the cities of Essen and Berlin. He knew exactly how he wanted 'his' bombers to be employed, resisting demands from the Army and the Navy, and from those who demanded attacks on what he called 'Panacea targets'. Harris was determined to attack the morale of the civilian population, and especially the industrial workers, and wanted to attack Germany's capacity to actually wage war.

His efforts to expand Bomber Command gradually bore fruit, although he did suffer setbacks. During 1942, for example, he was forced to stand by and watch the transfer of three Whitley, two Wellington and one Hampden squadron to Coastal Command.

'R-Robert' was lost on 2/3 October 1942 during an attack on Flensburg. No 405 Sqn subsequently transferred to No 8 Group, becoming the second Pathfinder Halifax unit (*via Aeroplane*)

The '*RUHR VALLEY EXPRESS*' is seen here in flight. No 405 Sqn made its first attack on 30/31 May 1942, participating in the first historic 1000 Bomber Raid against Köln (*via Phil Jarrett*)

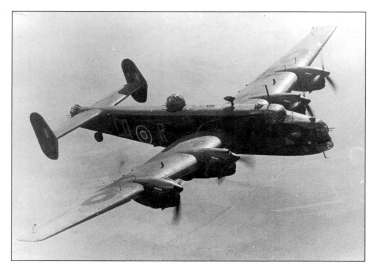

In so many ways the 'engine that won the War', the Rolls-Royce Merlin was always 'second-best' in the Handley Page Halifax, which only really flourished when refitted with the radials its designers' had always wanted. Here, 'erks' work on the engines of a B II in the open, as they so often had to (*via Aeroplane*)

Battle damage to a No 158 Sqn Halifax B II Series I Special, inflicted during a raid on Köln on 28 June 1943 (*via Dr Alfred Price*)

As the aircraft destined to overshadow the Halifax forever, the Lancaster commenced operations on 3 March 1942. From the beginning, the bomber showed great promise, and soon outshone the original Merlin-powered Halifax. The Lancaster's excellence should not have been unexpected, for after the disastrous record of the Manchester, the new four-engined 'heavy' represented a second chance for Avro to 'get it right', for many of the factors which limited the performance of the Halifax and Manchester (the 100-ft maximum wingspan stipulation and the requirement that the aircraft be capable of fulfilling other roles) were waived when the Lancaster was designed.

Had Handley Page been given the same unrestricted freedom as Avro when it drew up the Halifax, things might have been very different. Indeed, even the Halifax B VI, with only the extended span wings, was probably a better all-rounder than any Lancaster variant.

March 1942 was a 'slack month' for the Halifax force, which was briefly screened from operations while its aircraft were fitted with the new *Gee* (Ground Electronics Equipment) navigation aid. The aircraft were back in action before the month was out, however, when Halifaxes participated in the 234-strong bomber raid on Lubeck on

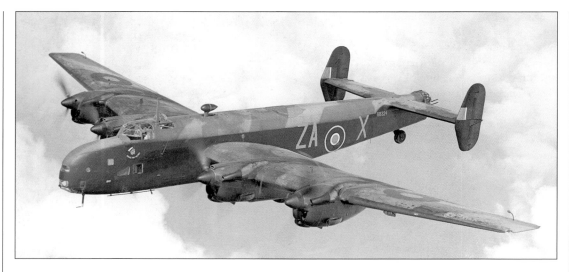

28/29 March. An old German city, Lubeck contained a high proportion of wooden buildings, and 62 per cent of these were burned out in the RAF's first 'Fire Raid' of the war. The attack was a profound psychological shock to the Nazi regime, and directly provoked the so-called 'Baedeker raids' (named after the famous German guide books, and aimed against Britain's most historic, and beautiful, towns).

On 30 March 34 Halifaxes again set out to attack the *Tirpitz* in its Norwegian refuge. The attack was again foiled by low cloud, and six aircraft failed to return. Two more attacks were made on 27 and 28 April, with 32 aircraft on the first day (four of which were lost) and 24 on the second (two falling). On the 27th, one of the casualties was none other than No 10 Sqn's new CO, Wg Cdr Bennett, who successfully escaped his stricken bomber and evaded to neutral Sweden. He was back with his unit within a month.

In April, Bomber Command also finally gained a fourth Halifax squadron, No 102, which had flown its last Whitley mission at the end of January, and whose conversion had been unusually protracted. A reasonably good month was rounded off by publication of the Singleton report, which assessed that bombing represented good 'value-for-money'.

Heavy losses led to radical measures to improve performance. The B II Series I (Special) had the nose turret (and often the mid-upper) removed and faired over, as seen in this view of a No 10 Sqn aircraft, named *'Wings for Victory'* (*via* Aeroplane)

Operations staff signal the pilot of this No 102 Sqn B II Series I (Special) to make ready for take-off. His aircraft is fitted with the streamlined 'Tollerton' nose, but retains its mid-upper gun turret. No 102 operated from Dalton, Topcliffe and Pocklington, flying a succession of Halifax variants (*via* Bruce Robertson)

May 1942 was a historic month for Bomber Command, with the issue of a new directive on 5 May calling for attacks on the German aircraft industry – Augsburg, Leipzig, Regensburg, Warnemunde and Wiener Neustadt were now targeted. But Harris was against specific targeting, and had had his prejudices confirmed (at least in his own mind) by the failure of the Augsburg raid in mid April. This had cost seven of the 12 participating Lancasters (and 49 aircrew), and yet had caused little damage to the Messerschmitt factory. His answer was to overwhelm area targets with massive force, with the primary aim of causing widespread destruction and mass panic among the populace. He began planning for a 1000 Bomber Raid – an ambitious aim at a time when mass raids tended to mean 160 or 230 aircraft.

On the 30/31 May, Harris launched the first 1000 Bomber Raid against Köln. Originally planned for 27 May 1942, the raid was postponed due to poor weather. The force of 1047 bombers included large numbers of aircraft from Operational Training Units (OTUs) and even a handful from Training Command, and was dominated by elderly twin-engined types. There were, for instance, no less than 602 Wellingtons involved, together with 28 Whitleys and 45 Hampdens. To these were added 46 Manchesters, 88 Stirlings, 73 Lancasters and 131 Halifaxes – still the most numerous of the 'heavies'. This total included aircraft from two newly-formed Halifax units, No 78 Sqn and the Canadian-manned No 405 Sqn, and from No 1652 Heavy Conversion Unit.

Some 41 of the attacking aircraft were lost, four of them Halifaxes, with 4.8 per cent losses in the first wave, 4.1 per cent in the second and only 1.9 per cent in the final wave. Some 868 aircraft actually bombed the target. Civilian casualties in Köln were remarkably light, with only 411 being killed. But the city had been singularly well-prepared for the raid through the provision of 500 public air raid shelters and 75,000 private shelters for its 75,000 inhabitants. However, although human casualties were light, destruction was horrific and widespread, and 25 per cent of the populace fled the city in the next few days.

Eight Halifaxes were lost on the second 1000 Bomber Raid on 1/2 June 1942 against Essen. No 76 Sqn marked the target on this, and the third 1000 Bomber Raid against Bremen on 25/26 June – six Halifaxes were lost that night.

A Halifax roars in over the village sports ground at an unnamed Yorkshire aerodrome. The official caption was headlined 'HALIFAXES LEAVE HERE TO WIPE OUT GERMAN WAR INDUSTRY'. At this difficult phase of the war, many failed to return (*via Phil Jarrett*)

This No 158 Sqn Halifax was one of many that failed to return. Lost on the 8 November 1942, the aircraft saved most of its crew, however. A surprisingly high number of Halifax aircrew survived being shot down, especially in comparison with their counterparts in the 'Lanc' (*via Phil Jarrett*)

The 1000 Bomber Raids saw some use of 4000-lb and 8000-lb bombs by the Halifax, following the first operational use of the 8000-lb bomb by No 76 Sqn on 11 April.

By the end of June there was increasing concern about the heavy loss rate suffered by the Halifax (5.3 per cent), which was attributed to the aircraft's poorly-shrouded exhausts. These made the aircraft easier for German nightfighters (see *Osprey Aircraft of the Aces 19 - German Nightfighter Aces of World War 2* for further details) to acquire. Later in the year, recommendations were made that Halifax pilots should fly between three and five sorties as 'Second Dickie', or against lightly defended targets, before being committed to the assault on Germany. There was a suspicion that inexperienced pilots were nervous of the Halifax, whose handling characteristics were tricky in some parts of the envelope. This tended to be borne out by the fact that the lost rate among experienced Halifax crews was far lower than for experienced crews of other types.

A sixth Halifax unit flew its first operation on 1 September, but as a No 1 Group squadron, it re-equipped with Lancasters at the end of October so as to allow all Handley Page bombers to be concentrated within No 4 Group. The second Royal Canadian Air Force (RCAF) unit, No 408 Sqn, to equip with the Halifax received B Vs during October, this new variant being fitted with a Dowty lever suspension undercarriage which should have marked a considerable improvement over the original Messier unit. Unfortunately, the Dowty landing gear used poorly-manufactured castings, and weight restrictions were soon imposed on the B V.

More significant than the arrival of the B V was the delivery of the first B I Series I (Special), which had a streamlined fairing fitted in place of the nose turret. This gave improved performance and range, and reduced the vulnerability of the aircraft. These 'Specials' were heavily committed to the raids against Italian targets, which commenced in the final months of 1942.

The Halifax B I Series IA introduced a nose that was both streamlined and transparent, and which could even mount a single machine gun in a low-drag mounting. This was a welcome development, since the Series I (Specials) had become vulnerable to frontal attacks. This aircraft served with No 51 Sqn at Snaith (*via Jerry Scutts*)

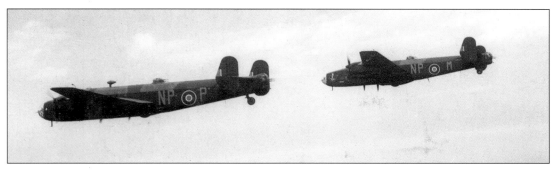

A pair of No 158 Sqn B II Series IAs in flight. The furthest aircraft (HR719) was lost on 11/12 June 1943 during a raid on Dusseldorf (*via Phil Jarrett*)

There was an optimistic start to 1943. Bomber Command, under its new C-in-C, had survived 1942, and had started to make some progress, but in 1943 it would start inflicting real damage on the enemy. The PFF was raised to Group status on 1 January, and a new Canadian Bomber Group (No 6) was formed at the same time. Bomber Command was now ready to start a true strategic air campaign, although it was initially diverted by the U-boat crisis, which forced a concentration on attacking the virtually bomb-proof U-boat pens in the submarines' French coast home-ports.

But the diversion, while unnecessary, was relatively short-lived, for on 16 January Bomber Command raided Berlin for the first time since 1941. Three Lancasters dropped flares to allow five Halifaxes and five Lancasters to mark the target for the Main Force bombers which followed. Seventeen Halifaxes accompanied 170 Lancasters on the second Berlin raid on 17 January, with three Halifaxes being among the 22 aircraft lost. At the end of the month, on 30/31 January, H2S made its first operational appearance during the raid on Hamburg. But production of H2S was slow, and fewer than 18 aircraft in each raid carried the equipment until late into the summer.

In February the Lancaster finally overtook the Halifax as being numerically the most important type in Bomber Command's inventory. The frontline establishment of 1091 aircraft included 642 'heavies', with 295 Lancasters, 228 Halifaxes and 119 Stirlings.

The Ruhr was Germany's most important industrial area, and with the introduction of *Gee* and H2S, it fell within easy reach of Bomber Command's 'heavies'. The Battle of the Ruhr Valley began on 5/6 March,

The last B II Series IAs added the rectangular tailfins normally associated with Hercules-engined Halifaxes, as seen on this No 78 Sqn aeroplane (*via Bruce Robertson*)

with *Mandrel* making an appearance jamming German *Freya* early warning radar, and with the bombers' IFF sets being used to jam *Würzburg*. The huge Krupp steel works received a thorough 'pasting', suffering ten per cent damage.

On 16/17 April Bomber Command attempted to attack the Skoda Works at Pilsen, but was largely unsuccessful, with some 18 Halifaxes and 18 Lancasters (of 327 despatched) failing to return. As Bomber Command continued to pound away at German industry, a Combined Bomber Offensive (*Pointblank*) was proposed, with 76 precise targets, to prepare the way for the eventual invasion of occupied Europe. Priority targets were submarine construction and bases, the German aircraft industry, ball-bearings and the oil industry. This target list was later re-prioritised, with German fighters added to the top of the list, and with synthetic rubber production and military Motor Transport added below oil.

June 1943 saw the introduction of *Monica*, an active tail warning receiver with a range of about four miles. In a densely packed bomber stream, the equipment was subject to a very high 'false warning' rate, and the Germans soon developed *Flensburg*, a device which allowed German nightfighters to home onto *Monica*'s transmissions. The Summer of 1943 saw a pendulum of 'measure' and countermeasure as Bomber Command and the German nightfighter arm struggled to gain the upper hand.

The introduction of *Gee* had allowed Bomber Command to compress and tighten the 'bomber stream', feeding hundreds of aircraft over their target within a short space of time. German defences consisted of a continuous

The arid North African climate, blowing sand and high temperatures, all represented difficult conditions for men and machines accustomed to more temperate climes. The nearest Halifax in this picture shows only too clearly the abrasive effects of blowing sand and dust as its sits waiting for its crew. But the Halifax performed very well in the desert, and later in India (*via* Aeroplane)

This Halifax of No 462 Sqn is seen high over the featureless wastes of the Western Desert, en route on a 'Mail Run' bombing mission to Benghazi. The aircraft was lost in a take-off accident on 29 September 1942, from which the crew fortunately escaped (*via Bruce Robertson*)

belt of GCI radar stations (each with three radars) arranged in a belt of boxes, two deep, known as the *Himmelbett*. Each box could control a single fighter at a time, guiding it onto individually-tracked targets. This almost guaranteed a kill, although the controllers could thus easily be swamped if a bomber stream poured through 'their' box.

July 1943 saw the launch of Operation *Gomorrah* against Hamburg, with 791 bombers (including 246 Halifaxes) attacking on 24/25 July. Only four of the Halifaxes were lost thanks to the use of a new radar countermeasure. Bomber Command used *Window* for the first time during this raid, dispersing clouds of thin strips of foil to provide 'false' echoes which effectively blinded German early warning radar. This rendered the *Himmelbett* even less effective, and the system was replaced. German controllers and airborne and ground-based observers began tracking the whole stream, transmitting a 'running commentary' as to its progress, course, airspeed and altitude. Free ranging *'Wilde Sau'* fighters then picked their own targets, sometimes aided by high flying Ju 88s which dropped flares to illuminate the bombers.

This tactic meant that the bombers came under attack not only as they transited through the coastal belt, and over the target itself, but all the way from the coast to the target and back. Despite this, *Window* was generally judged to have been a useful measure, and allowed dummy or 'spoof' raids to be flown which often drew nightfighters away from the Main Force.

On the ground, the raids on Hamburg were no less significant. A second attack on 27/28 July caused an intense conflagration (the famous 'Firestorm') which killed an estimated 40,000 people, destroyed three-quarters of the city and caused two-thirds of the population to flee before the third raid on 29/30 July.

August saw Bomber Command proving that it could hit precision targets with just as much effect. In Operation *Hydra*, on 17/18 August, Bomber Command struck the research station at Peenemünde with overwhelming force, using the Master Bomber technique for the first time. Destruction was enormous, although two Halifaxes from No 8 Group failed to return, together with three from No 4 Group and ten from No 6 Group. The attacks were carried out from fairly low level (4000 ft), so there was a relatively poor survival rate among the crews of the aircraft that were lost.

The aftermath of another take-off accident in the desert, as No 462 Sqn's 'K-Kitty' waits to be stripped for useable spares at El Daba in December 1942 (*via Phil Jarrett*)

Aircraft losses reached a similarly alarming level during the 23/24 August attack on Berlin, with six of 34 PFF Halifaxes being shot down, and overall Halifax losses representing ten per cent of the aircraft despatched. The Stirling fared even

worse, with 13 per cent of the aircraft despatched failing to return. Overall, 56 of the 727 bombers sortied were lost, representing 7.9 per cent of the force.

By October, H2S was coming on stream, with 155 Halifaxes, 70 Stirlings and 225 Lancasters having been delivered with the equipment fitted. Normal attrition had already wiped out 70 of the H2S-equipped Halifaxes, together with 50 of the Lancasters and 29 of the Stirlings, but replacement H2S aircraft were by now pouring off the production lines. Bomber Command's Main Force was by then all four-engined, the Manchester having disappeared after the 25/26 June attack on Bremen, and with the Wellington having flown its last pure bombing mission on 8/9 October. By the time Bomber Command launched the Battle of Berlin, the bombing force consisted solely of Mosquitos (see *Osprey Combat Aircraft 4 – Mosquito Bomber/Fighter-Bomber Units of World War 2* for further details) and 'heavies', and 90 per cent of the Lancasters, Halifaxes and Stirlings had H2S equipment fitted.

Wellingtons still remained on Bomber Command's books, of course, with training units and with the Elint squadrons which constituted the new No 100 Group, which officially formed on 23 November 1943. No 100 Group was initially equipped with a variety of aircraft types, including Mosquitos, B-17s and Stirlings, although the Halifax would eventually become the group's work-horse.

The year ended badly for Bomber Command, with the Battle of Berlin underlining an unacceptably high loss rate, and raising questions as to the C-in-C's judgement. After implacable opposition to 'side-show operations', and high profile raids driven more by political expedience and public relations requirements, Harris appeared to have fallen into the trap of undertaking operations which some felt amounted to 'Gesture Warfare'. Rather than concentrating on targets in Western parts of Germany, Harris was seduced by the perceived need to hit the Nazi capital, although it was too far away, was a poor H2S target, and was too heavily defended.

Air- and groundcrew of No 462 Sqn pose in front of one of the unit's ageing Halifax B IIs during August 1943 (*via Phil Jarrett*)

No 462 Sqn's Halifaxes were eventually locally-modified to B II Series I (Special) standards, as seen here. The aircraft provided the Desert Air Force with an invaluable long-range striking tool (*via Phil Jarrett*)

A No 462 Sqn Halifax taxies at a forward base, instantly creating its own miniature sandstorm. Four more of the squadron's aircraft wait to follow it (*via Phil Jarrett*)

The first phase of the Battle of Berlin took place between 18 November and 3 December, but was disrupted by poor weather and by the ineffectiveness of H2S over a city which had few really good radar features. The loss rate suffered by the Stirling was sufficient to see it withdrawn from all operations over Germany.

Between 16 December and 3 January 1944, the Battle of Berlin entered its second phase. This was mainly an all-Lancaster show, although 250 Halifaxes were among the 700 bombers despatched on 29/30 December. The mission marked the first mass raid by Halifaxes for a month, and the aircraft failed to re-visit Berlin until 20/21 January 1944, when the RAF's 35 losses included no fewer than 22 Halifaxes. The second phase ran from 20 to 31 January and the fourth from 15 February to 25 March.

NORTH AFRICAN SIDE-SHOW

While the main role of the Halifax during 1942-43 was in contributing to the Bomber Command offensive against Germany, the aircraft was also

active elsewhere and in other roles, most notably over the North African desert.

By June 1942, the war in North Africa was going badly, and major elements (16 aircraft each) from two Halifax squadrons – Nos 10 and 76 – were detached to Aqir, in Palestine. Under Operation *Barefaced*, the 'short term' detachment was ostensibly made for a mission against the Italian fleet, although on arrival, aircrew realised that theirs was a long-term commitment to the Desert Air Force.

The Halifaxes formed No 249 Wing within No 205 Group, and immediately began flying long-range attacks against Tobruk and Benghazi. The detachment suffered its first loss on 13/14 July, during a mission to Tobruk.

Rommel's offensive failed in September, largely due to fuel shortages. This caused the Desert Air Force to redouble its efforts against Rommel's supply chain, and the Halifaxes naturally played their part in this effort. On 5 September eight aircraft (a ninth aborted after take-off) attacked Heraklion airfield on the island of Crete. Two of the Halifaxes were downed by flak over the target, and another was damaged by a pair of intercepting Bf 109s.

The two separate detachments were ordered to merge on 6 September, amalgamating to form No 462 Sqn – nominally an RAAF unit, although relatively few 'Aussies' served with the squadron. Tobruk continued to be the main target for the Halifaxes, but Crete also came under attack again in October. That month also saw the Halifaxes tasked with close support missions in advance of the Battle of El Alamein, including night strafing attacks from as low as 1200 ft.

Attention switched to Sicily in late January 1943, and then to German airfields in southern Italy. The No 462 Sqn Halifaxes suffered a spate of engine problems and engine failures in April, and in response, the aircraft had their nose and mid-upper gun turrets removed to reduce weight and drag, and thereby ease the load on the hard-worked Merlins. Replacement aircraft with Merlin 22 engines arrived in the late summer.

No 178 Sqn re-equipped with Halifaxes in May, and flew its first operation on 31 May, before reverting to Liberators in September. No 462 Sqn received its first H2S-equipped aircraft in January 1944, and moved to Celone, Italy, in February. Here, it was re-numbered as No 614 Sqn, and went on to attack targets in France, Austria, Germany, Italy and the Balkans.

Although the majority of its missions saw the unit performing target marking for other No 205 Group squadrons in-theatre, No 614 Sqn also frequently undertook supply dropping and 'straight' bombing sorties as well. The unit flew its final Halifax operation of the war on 3 March 1945.

Although living conditions for the air- and groundcrews of No 462 Sqn were often primitive, the flying was better than in Europe, with less danger from flak and fighters, although it was still a dangerous and challenging job (*via Phil Jarrett*)

BREAKING THE BACK OF THE REICH

The seeds of victory in the bomber war were sowed in 1943, and that year ended with the percentage loss rate plummeting. But in other respects, 1943 ended badly, with the Battle of Berlin proving a hugely expensive drain on Bomber Command. Indeed, the actual numbers of aircraft lost were never higher than in late 1943.

However, the foundations for better times for the Halifax squadrons had already been laid, and the Hercules-engined B III began to arrive in November 1943, with Nos 433 and 466 Sqns being the first to re-equip. The latter unit carried out the first operational mission with the bomber on 1 December, sending a dozen aircraft (along with 19 Stirlings) on a coastal mining mission off the Frisian islands. None were lost – a good start. Nine squadrons of B IIIs were operational by mid-January, representing a significant proportion of the Main Force.

It had been planned that the B IIIs would all enter service with H2S fitted, but there was a grave shortage of sets, and from February 1944, significant numbers were completed instead with a ventral Preston-Green turret, boasting a single 0.50-in gun. Some units made further improvements, No 431 Sqn, for example, installing a second gun in the turret.

January 1944 saw Halifax losses (which were already proportionally higher than those of the Lancaster) rising to an all time peak. During the month, No 4 Group suffered a loss rate of 11.4 per cent in sorties against targets in Germany, and things were no better in other groups. No 434

Halifax B II Series I (Special) R9534 served as the B III prototype, and originally retained triangular fins and the 'tall' mid-upper gun turret, although these features were replaced (*Author's Collection*)

Although it wears the distinctive yellow 'prototype' marking, HX238 was an early-production B III retained for trials at Boscombe Down, and not the prototype. It is seen here with Hercules 100 engines, acting as a B VI prototype (*Author's Collection*)

Installation of the Hercules transformed the Halifax, although many of those in authority were slow to catch up with the fact, and the aircraft continued to be viewed as a second-best to the Lancaster (*via Phil Jarrett*)

Sqn was hit worst of all, with a 24.2 per cent wastage. On 19/20 January, 823 aircraft set out against Leipzig and 78 failed to return. This was quite bad enough, but 34 of the missing aircraft were Halifaxes – a significant 14.9 per cent chunk of the Halifax force that had set out.

Two days later, on 21/22 January, 57 of 648 bombers despatched to Magdeburg went missing, including 35 of the 224 Halifaxes. This represented a staggering loss rate of 15.6 per cent. The remaining Merlin-powered Halifaxes (with Nos 10, 77, 102, and 419 Sqns) had taken the biggest pounding, and the January losses led to their withdrawal from Main Force operations against German targets, although the variant continued to operate over Germany with the PFF and No 100 Group.

Bomber Command's campaign continued unabated throughout February and March 1944 as the Battle of Berlin raged, with the heaviest attack being flown on 15/16 February when 891 aircraft sortied. Targets in Augsburg, Stuttgart and Schweinfurt were also hit, with the raid on the latter city being carried out in two parts. The initial wave of 392 aircraft lost 22 aircraft, and the second wave of 342 had 11 bombers downed – seven of these were Halifaxes. The attacks carried out that night were deemed to be a great success, with both Berlin and Augsburg being thoroughly devastated. But the successes here could not compensate for the disaster that was the last major attack on Berlin of the war.

On 24/25 March Bomber Command despatched 811 aircraft against the German capital, 216 of them Halifaxes. Strong winds scattered the

bomber stream, and some 50 aircraft were shot down by unerringly accurate flak and 14 more by nightfighters, while the fate of the remaining eight aircraft which failed to return cannot be accurately assigned. Twenty-eight of the 72 losses were Halifaxes – one of the heaviest loss rates to befall the type. Stronger-than-forecast winds had scattered the force, and many strayed across the heavily defended Ruhr valley on their return journey.

Many suspect that Victoria Crosses have often been more easily won during military disasters, and some have inferred that the award has sometimes been a propaganda tool, being used to snatch some glory from what might otherwise have been remembered as an inglorious failure. Such a suggestion is probably unfair, however compelling the theory might sound. Certainly the name of Nuremberg has become synonymous with one of Bomber Command's bitterest defeats in the long and bloody bomber war.

The 30 March 1944 raid against Nuremberg was a 'Maximum Effort', a mass raid against a target 600 miles inside Germany, and one which involved sending the bombers past, or over, countless other heavily-defended targets. Nuremberg itself was also a relatively heavily defended city, yet to 'Bomber' Harris it was a useful target, not only because it was an important node in the German transport and communications network. Nuremberg was to many the tokenistic birthplace and shrine of the Third Reich (for the part it played in pre-war rallies), and a successful attack would be a useful demonstration that 'no-where was safe'. But the attack was one against an ancient city of minor industrial importance.

Harris despatched 572 Lancasters, 214 Halifaxes and nine Mosquitoes against Nuremberg, and of these, 64 Lancasters and 31 Halifaxes failed to return. Five more of each were so badly damaged that they were written off after landing, and 59 aircraft were damaged. This represented 12.1 per cent of the Lancasters despatched, and 16.8 per cent of the Halifaxes. Inaccurate weather forecasts had seen the force blown miles off course and scattered, making accurate attacks impossible, and rendering the

Unpainted cowl flaps and cowlings on these Halifaxes probably indicate that they were photographed following depot-level repairs. Quite badly damaged aircraft were sometimes salvaged and fitted with extensive new sub-assemblies. NA695, for example, retained little more than its tail unit and rear fuselage, gaining a new forward fuselage, wing control surfaces and engines, and thus becoming a B VII in the process (*via Phil Jarrett*)

Only the individual aircraft letter 'A' can be discerned on this anonymous B III from an equally unknown Bomber Command squadron. A tractor is just driving away, perhaps having towed the aircraft to its dispersal (*via Phil Jarrett*)

It is uncertain whether MZ359 was photographed before the application of full squadron codes, or whether these were removed by the wartime censor. Two-letter identity codes were usually applied in frontline Bomber Command units, but were less common in Coastal Command and SOE units (*via Phil Jarrett*)

bombers even more vulnerable to enemy fighters. Some 80 aircraft were lost en route to the target, and 55 more aborted and turned for home. Of the remainder, more than 100 aircraft mistakenly bombed Schweinfurt instead, others scattered their bombs far and wide, and a handful pressed on to find Nuremberg swathed in cloud. Damage to the city was accordingly light. The raid was such a failure that it forced an end to mass attacks against major targets for some months, but (perhaps conveniently) the failure was accompanied by some glory.

Among the Halifaxes turned out to raid Nuremberg was the LK797 'E' of Flg Off Cyril Barton, who was a member of the newly-formed No 578 Sqn at Burn. Young, and relatively inexperienced, having notched up only 18 previous missions, Barton was also deeply religious – far from the caricature of a Bomber Command pilot. He knelt beside his bed in prayer every night, confided in letters home that he was worried that his witness was 'not vigorous enough', and reported on the progress of his attempts to 'convert' his crew. But Barton's piety did not save him from danger.

Turning towards Nuremberg, a Ju 88 and an Me 410 made head-on attacks against his aircraft, puncturing two fuel tanks, putting the rear turret out of action, knocking out the radio and intercom and setting the starboard inner engine on fire. More passes saw further hits scored, and during these the navigator, bomb-aimer and wireless operator bailed out, having mistaken the gunner's morse instructions to corkscrew right ('Dot Dash Dot, R') for the instruction to bail out ('Dot Dash Dash Dot, P').

Barton, characteristically, pressed on, and seems to have been one of those who bombed Schweinfurt. Running out of fuel, the engines stopped, and with the aircraft too low to be abandoned, Barton was obliged to make a forced landing as dawn was breaking, a few minutes before 0600 on 31 March. The aircraft hit houses in the coastal village of Ryhope (south of Sunderland), demolished a railway footbridge, killed a miner on his way to work and finally came to rest, the rear fuselage

With H2S and the low-slung Bristol B12 mid-upper turret, this Halifax B III looks considerably more modern than the B IIs which had been common only a few months before (*via Phil Jarrett*)

breaking off and falling into the railway cutting. The three remaining crew in the rear fuselage were dazed, but survived, and Barton himself was conscious when he was dragged from the wreckage of the cockpit, but died on reaching hospital. His posthumous VC was awarded in June 1944.

After Nuremberg, Bomber Command switched its attention to tactical bombing in preparation for the invasion of occupied Europe – a campaign which had begun earlier in March, with experimental raids against French and Belgian railway marshalling yards. Operational control of Bomber Command passed to SHAEF on 14 April, and on 17 April, Air Chief Marshal Sir Arthur Tedder issued a directive assigning the Command to attacks against enemy fighters, and railways, as well as continuing to disorganise German industry. Attacks against German targets also served the dual purpose of keeping nightfighters tied to their bases.

Having to fly over enemy territory for relatively short periods, Bomber Command experienced only light losses during these tactical raids, and achieved extraordinary accuracy against French targets. Because crews executed individually-aimed attacks against targets marked by Pathfinders, they were far more accurate than the USAAF's day bombers, who bombed 'on command' in combat boxes from higher altitude. This was fortunate, since the need to avoid collateral damage to French civilians

A No 426 Sqn Halifax B III falls in flames near Munchen Gladbach on 24 March 1945, its demise being photographed from a No 408 Sqn aircraft (*via Phil Jarrett*)

After serving in North Africa with Halifax B IIs, No 462 Sqn reformed at Driffield within No 4 Group and operated as a Main Force bomber unit until December 1944, when it joined No 100 Group. B IIs gave way to B IIIs in August 1944. Many photos of the squadron's initial B IIIs had the H2S or ventral Preston-Green turrets removed by the censor (*via Bruce Robertson*)

No 77 Sqn was a No 4 Group Halifax unit which converted to the B III in May 1944, having previously operated B IIs and B Vs. This aircraft carries H2S and *Monica* (*via Bruce Robertson*)

This Halifax served with the 'Francophone' No 425 (*Alouette*) Sqn, and is seen here on 27 November 1944 being waved off on a mission to Neuss from Tholthorpe. The aircraft carries a single 0.50-in machine gun in its ventral Preston-Green turret (*via Bruce Robertson*)

was felt to be extremely important.

The Halifaxes of Nos 4 and 6 Groups played a disproportionate part in the spring offensive against these targets, with the overall campaign involving some 4428 Halifax sorties, and the loss of only 99 aircraft – a loss rate of below 0.5 per cent. Aircraft typically carried nine 1000-lb and six 500-lb bombs on these missions.

Losses were heavier when the Halifaxes hit railway yards in Germany itself, however, with 14 of the aircraft downed falling during the raid on Montzen on 27/28 April, followed by a further 18 during the attack on Aachen on 24/25 May. But overall, the campaign was considered to be a success, and was expanded. Eighty targets were identified, and 37 of these were allocated to RAF Bomber Command, with the remainder assigned to the USAAF's Ninth Air Force, 2 ATAF and Fighter Command.

By the time of the invasion, 51 of the targets had been heavily damaged and a further 25 severely damaged, thus dramatically restricting the mobility of German forces as they tried to respond to D-Day. The last attack was made against Trappes marshalling yards on 2/3 June, although on this occasion nightfighters destroyed 16 of the 128 bombers sortied.

In addition to the attacks against the French railway system, Bomber Command continued to strike at targets associated with the enemy's aircraft industry, as well troop concentrations and camps. They also mounted attacks intended to disrupt the German early warning system, and against fortified coastal defences (Hitler's 'West Wall'), although these were less successful.

Even after the invasion, Bomber Command continued to be committed to operations in support of the Allied armies. Bridges and railway junctions were hit, often at relatively low level (2000 to 3000 ft), and because these targets were usually further inland, losses rose accordingly. The only attacks against targets in Germany during this time were made on oil targets.

Between 16 June and 31 August the Halifaxes were also heavily committed to operations against the flying bomb (*Noball*) sites. From 22 June, these included a number of daylight raids, with anti-*Noball* missions usually involving between 150 and 200 Halifaxes per mission. Some missions, however, saw as many as 492 Halifaxes sortied.

Although these numbers were highly impressive, each mission usually saw roughly 50 per cent more Lancasters despatched, and these suffered considerably higher losses accordingly – 49 Avro bombers were shot down compared with just two Halifaxes.

The Preston-Green turret usually mounted a single 0.50-in machine gun, although a number of squadrons used a twin-gun mounting, as seen here (*via Dr Alfred Price*)

Harris and others fumed as invasion support sorties continued on well into the summer of 1944. He was impatient to get back to the strategic bombing campaign, and was worried that German industry had been given a long breathing space in which to recuperate, relocate and strengthen its defences. When it did return to the fray, Bomber Command's Halifax force had changed. The last Merlin-engined aircraft left Nos 102 and 77 Sqns in May and June, although the B II/V did not fully disappear until July, since the newly-forming Free French units used both variants until they could gain sufficient B IIIs. It is believed that these units flew only one operation with the Merlin-engined B II/V, however.

As the B II/V left service, the new B VII entered the fray. The interim Hercules XVI-engined aircraft re-equipped Nos 426 and 432 Sqns from 16 and 20 June, with No 408 following in July.

On 8 July, Bomber Command Halifaxes participated in close air support operations mounted to aid Gen Montgomery's frontal assault on Caen, following attacks by Lancasters alone the previous day. Similar attacks (to allow an Allied breakout) were flown on 18 July as part of Operation *Goodwood*, bombs being dropped within half a mile of British forward positions. Bomber Command flew several more close support operations, culminating in Operation *Tractable* on 14 August, in which bombs fell within 2000 yards of Canadian troops.

The Strategic Bombing Offensive re-opened on 23/24 July 1944 with an attack against Kiel. This was Bomber Command's first attack against a German city for two months, and of 629 aircraft

The ventral gunner's seat and turret controls of a Halifax B III fitted with the Preston-Green turret (*via Dr Alfred Price*)

OSCAR was one of the most colourful Halifaxes within the Canadian No 6 Group, where gaudy nose-art became increasingly common in late 1944 and early 1945. The aircraft is seen here setting off for a mission (its 58th) on 13 November 1944 whilst still in service with No 424 ('Tiger') Sqn at Skipton-on-Swale. It later transferred to No 187 Sqn (*via Phil Jarrett*)

A close-up of the nose-art worn by No 51 Sqn's *EXPENSIVE BABE*, which is the subject of one of the colour plates in this volume. Several Snaith-based aircraft wore similar artwork, which was presumably the work of the same talented individual (*via Bruce Robertson*)

despatched, only four failed to return (all of them Lancasters) – no Halifax was brought down, although German defences were soon awake, and subsequent raids met stiffer resistance.

The offensive gathered pace later in the month, with attacks on Stuttgart and Hamburg, and on a number of synthetic oil plants. Another notable raid was made on 12/13 August, when 287 Halifaxes and Lancasters targeted Opel's V1 assembly plant at Russelheim. Twenty of the attackers failed to return. The war on the V1 finally ended in September, when the last launch sites on the Pas de Calais were finally overrun. On 17 August, 1004 bombers attacked nine nightfighter airfields in Belgium and the Netherlands, helping to clear the way for a return to intensive night bombing ops over Germany.

Operational control of Bomber Command reverted to the Air Ministry (from SHAEF) on 14 September 1944, and Harris regained much of the autonomy he had enjoyed before signing 'his' bombers over to Gen Eisenhower, and his air commander, Tedder. He was still expected to operate in support of the advancing Allied armies when required, however. For example, on 25 September 70 Halifaxes of Nos 77, 102, 346 and 347 Sqns delivered fuel to Melsbroek for the army, each aircraft carrying 165 jerrycans. September also saw attacks against isolated German fortresses at Le Havre, Boulogne and Calais, forcing their early surrender.

U-boats pens on the Norwegian coast were attacked on 4 October, 47 No 8 Group Lancasters leading 93 No 6 Group Halifaxes to the target – these had proven vital to the Germans following the loss of French bases.

Bomber Command launched Operation *Hurricane* on 6/7 October with a major attack on Dortmund. Conducted as a demonstration of Allied air superiority, the operation involved bombing targets in the once formidable Ruhr round-the-clock. Loss rates had, by now, plummeted to one per cent or less, and such operations were easily sustainable.

In late October, Halifaxes were involved in attacks on the low-lying Walcheren Island in the Scheldt estuary. This fortified island was the gateway to Antwerp, and heavy bombing forced its surrender on 3 November. This removed another thorn in the Allies' rear.

Earlier that same month (on the 14th) a huge RAF heavy bomber force had struck Duisburg both during the day and at night, with Halifaxes being involved in both waves – 474 in the first attack (one of which failed to return) alone. Such was the ferocity of the raid that Bomber Command dropped a greater tonnage of bombs on Duisburg in one day than the Luftwaffe dropped on London during the whole war!

No 462 Sqn participated in the

daylight raid, when prowling German fighters shot down 15 of the attackers, and then returned by night, as part of yet another 1000 Bomber Raid. One of the squadron aircraft hit during the latter operation was the Halifax flown by Plt Off A J Cockerill, which suffered flak damage as it was lined up prior to the bombing run. Knocked unconscious, Cockerill came round, completed his attack and then set course for home. Despite the pain from his injuries, he refused morphine and struggled back to the UK, although the continual loss of blood made him progressively weaker. By the time he crossed the Kent coast he was nearly blind, and another crew member had to stand by him to call out the instrument readings. He landed safely at Manston, and survived the war. Other people won VCs for no more, but Cockerill's gallantry went largely unrecognised.

On 1 November 1944, Halifaxes downed a Messerschmitt Me 262 and an Me 163, the latter marking the only reported use of the German

The top-scoring Bomber Command Halifax was *'FRIDAY THE 13TH'*, seen here on display on the site of John Lewis's bombed-out store on Oxford Street. The aircraft retained the original Halifax 'square wingtips', although many B IIIs had extended round tips, like the B VI and B VII (*via Bruce Robertson*)

Seen in a wartime print sadly vandalised for use in a postwar publication, a No 346 Sqn Halifax is seen after the war flying past the Eiffel Tower. Bomber Command's two Free French Halifax units at Elvington were transferred back to French control in October 1945, along with their aircraft (*via* Aeroplane)

This No 38 Sqn B III was purchased by Mr G N Wickner and flown to Australia as G-AGXA, wearing new nose-art ('*Waltzing Matilda*'). Once in Australia, the aircraft was registered by owner's Air Carriers Ltd as VH-BDT. It was seen derelict at Mascot airport, in New South Wales, in 1947 (*via* Aeroplane)

rocket-propelled fighter at night. But even as late as November 1944, Halifaxes did not get things all their own way. On 4 November a raid against Bochum proved very costly, especially for the French-manned No 346 Sqn, which lost five of its 16 aircraft – these were among 23 Halifaxes which failed to return from the mission.

As the Allied armies raced forward, the target list steadily shrank. Accordingly, even before the German surrender, Bomber Command began to shrink, as the RAF prepared for the inevitable reductions which would accompany the peace. No 578 Sqn, for example, flew its last mission as early as 13 March 1945. But there was no real let-up, and 181,000 tons of bombs were dropped during the year – one-fifth of the total tonnage for the entire war.

Halifaxes continued to pound German industrial cities and communications hubs, but also provided bombardment of more tactical targets lying in the line of the Allied advance. The loss rate remained below one per cent, although when operational accidents were taken into account, this still meant that only two crews in three would survive a full frontline tour. German defences in the target area remained deadly, and crews also had to deal with the occasional threat of long-range night intruders.

A graphic demonstration of the Halifax's robustness came on 13/14 January when MZ465 of No 51 Sqn collided with another bomber. The aircraft lost a nine-foot section of its nose (containing the navigator and the bomb aimer) in the collision, leaving the cockpit open to a freezing blast of cold air. But despite the heavy damage, the pilot limped home and made a successful landing.

Even at this late stage in the war, Bomber Command continued to experiment with different ways of organising its attacks. On 16/17 January, for example, No 76 Sqn were sent in to attack the target *before* the PFF. Perhaps coincidentally, 17 of the 320 Halifaxes sent out that night failed to return.

The definitive Halifax B VI, with Hercules 100 engines, increased fuel tankage and a pressurised fuel system, finally entered frontline service and began operations over Germany (initially with No 102 Sqn) during

February 1945. By the end of the war, Halifax B VIs equipped five No 4 Group squadrons – Nos 76, 77, 346, 347 and 640.

The night of 3 March was a bad one for the Halifaxes of Nos 4 and 6 Groups. Although no enemy nightfighters were encountered over the target, seven aircraft were shot down around their own aerodromes. But this isolated action was little more than the death throes of the German nightfighter arm, and never again would they cause such carnage over the UK. The German fighters fought on with dogged determination, but losses soared, and fuel and spares shortages made life increasingly difficult for the enemy. Bomber Command had its only major daylight encounter with German jet fighters on 31 March, when 12 Me 262s of III./JG 7 tore into the bomber stream, downing three Halifaxes and five Lancasters using their cannon and R4M rockets.

Halifaxes played a part in Bomber Command's last major attack of the war, bombing coastal gun batteries at Wangerooge. Seven of the attacking bombers were lost (although six of these fell victim to air-to-air collisions) and only one enemy fighter (an Me 262) was even seen. This proved to be the last operation of the war for Nos 4 and 6 Groups.

The Hercules-engined Halifax proved as resilient as it was popular, and no less than four aircraft finished the war with more than 100 operational missions over Germany – LV937 with Nos 578 and 51 Sqns, LW587 and MZ527 with No 578 Sqn and LV907 with No 158 Sqn.

Once the German surrender had been signed on 7 May 1945, the Halifax force was quickly stood down. No 4 Group transferred to Transport Command and No 6 Group allocated eight squadrons to the Armies of Occupation. The aircraft were briefly kept busy dropping unwanted bomb stocks into the North Sea, and flying groundcrew on low-level sight-seeing tours of former German targets. The two French Halifax squadrons were duly presented to France, and soon the once prodigious Handley Page 'heavy' had become little more than a memory within Bomber Command.

B III LW125, bearing the name *'Sarie Marais'*, made a goodwill tour of South Africa following the successful completion of tropical trials at Khartoum (*via Phil Jarrett*)

This Halifax B VI is typical of the later version, with the Hercules 100 engines and extended, rounded, wingtips (*via Phil Jarrett*)

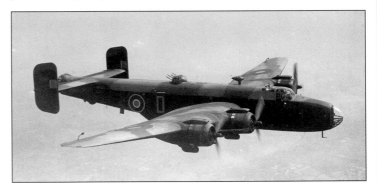

PATHFINDER FORCE

The RAF's 'pathfinder' concept, which saw an elite force of aircrew that had received specialised navigation training equipped with modified aircraft, was nothing new. Indeed, it was the success of the Luftwaffe's *Kampfgruppe* 100 during the Blitz on Britain in 1940–41 which had drawn Bomber Command's attention to the idea.

Bomber Command had been experimenting with the radio-based *Gee* navigation aid, which used three ground stations to allow the navigator to calculate his position by triangulation, since early 1942. It was useable on missions to the Ruhr, but as the bomber journeyed further east the radio pulses became weak and unreadable. It was probably most useful as an aid for finding the airfield on the return journey, but did allow the development of a basic target marking technique, known as 'Shaker'. This saw an initial wave of *Gee*-equipped aircraft dropping target illuminators, followed by a second wave (also *Gee*-equipped) dropping a maximum load of incendiaries, with the main force following and dropping HE.

Arthur Harris, as AOC-in-C Bomber Command, opposed the formation of a specialised group, which would have become a *corps d'elite* within his Command, preferring instead the idea of assigning each group's most successful squadron of the previous month to the target-marking role for a one-month period. He hoped that this would 'spread the load', foster healthy competition and prevent petty jealousies. Harris even opposed the forming of a single 'Pathfinding' or target marking squadron within each group. However, he was eventually instructed to set aside two Stirling and two Wellington units within No 3 Group for these tasks, although he resisted 'creaming off' of the best squadrons or crews.

Fortunately, Harris was persuaded to drop his opposition by the Directorate of Bomber Operations and a number of Pathfinder 'enthusiasts'. The most notable of the latter was Don Bennett, an extremely experienced long-range pilot and navigator who was promoted to group captain and appointed to command the Pathfinders on 5 July 1942, prior to its official establishment on 15 August 1942. Bennett remained at the helm of the force for the rest of the war, winning promotion to air commodore and then air vice marshal as the PFF increased in size and status. His 'drive, energy and relentless single-mindedness' were largely responsible for the PFF's success.

The force did initially consist of one squadron from each of the

An early Merlin XX-engined Halifax B II takes off, perhaps in the Mediterranean. The B II formed the initial equipment of No 35 Sqn after its transfer to the Pathfinder Force. The distinctive underwing landing light is clearly visible here (*via Phil Jarrett*)

frontline bomber groups, comprising No 156 Sqn with Wellingtons from No 1 Group, No 109 Sqn with Wellingtons and Mosquitos from No 2 Group, No 7 Sqn with Stirlings from No 3 Group, No 35 Sqn with Halifaxes from No 4 Group and No 83 Sqn with Lancasters from No 5 Group. The squadrons moved to adjacent airfields within No 3 Group (Warboys, Wyton, Oakington, Gravely and Wyton, respectively), however, and operated as a single elite force.

Bennett set high standards and sent crews which could not meet them to other Main Force squadrons, replacing them with hand-picked volunteers. Replacements were obtained by drawing the best crews from each group, and Bennett encouraged the growth of elitism, managing to gain authorisation for Pathfinder aircrew to wear a special badge below their normal flying brevet and medal ribbons.

No 8 (Path Finder Force) Group was officially formed as a group in its own right on 8 January 1943 – in time to lead Bomber Command's assault on the Ruhr. As the PFF expanded, it gained a second Halifax unit, No 405 'Vancouver' Sqn, RCAF, which moved in to Gransden Lodge in April 1943. The unit re-equipped with Lancasters in August 1943, followed by No 35 Sqn in March 1944.

The Halifax thus served for only 20 months within No 8 PFF Group, but performed very well, and actually suffered lower losses than the supposedly superior Lancaster. As PFF units, Nos 35 and 405 Sqns flew much the same missions as the Main Force units, and a full rundown of operations would thus be repetitive. Even a list of highlights would be too long for the format of this book!

However, it should be recorded that No 35 Sqn participated in the first Pathfinder Force attack against Flensburg on 18/19 August 1942. This

No 35 Sqn had already won something of a reputation for excellence and fighting spirit before its transfer to form part of the cadre of the Pathfinder Force in August 1942. Seen here during May 1942, W7676 was lost on 28/29 August 1942 during an attack on Nuremberg (*via Phil Jarrett*)

Armourers struggle with a bomb trolley – one of six waiting for loading of the 24 500-lb bombs aboard this Merlin XX-engined Halifax. Special, purpose-designed, target markers were soon developed for use by the Pathfinders, who also dropped incendiaries, and even continued to use some HE bombs like these (*via Phil Jarrett*)

The Halifax was well protected from above and behind, although Series IAs and B IIIs lacked forward-facing armament. The tiny stub below the rear turret is the antenna for the *Monica* radar warning receiver (*via Phil Jarrett*)

proved to be a poor start, since winds were not as forecast and the force was blown far north of its target. Some aircraft even attacked a town in Denmark! To add insult to injury, one of the four missing aircraft that night was a No 35 Sqn Halifax. The PFF's second raid, against Frankfurt on 24/25 August, was only marginally more successful, since the target was obscured by cloud.

The PFF finally showed what it could do against Kassel on 27/28 August, illuminating and bombing the target effectively, and the force finally demonstrated its value over Nuremburg on 28/29 August, marking the target with a new marker – 'Red Blob Fire'. But propaganda aside, accuracy improved very little until the PFF was able to deploy new radio and radar aids, and new target marking devices. But things started to change very rapidly at the beginning of 1943.

H2S made its operational debut over Hamburg on 30/31 January 1943, finally freeing the Pathfinders from reliance on *Gee*, and the limitations imposed by its ground stations. H2S was, in essence, a primitive ground-mapping radar, and its development was eagerly supported by Bennett. Test sets were delivered to No 35 Sqn (and to the Stirling-equipped No 7 Sqn) in December 1942, and these soon proved useful, especially against targets which had distinctive radar reflecting features such as large areas of water.

H2S demanded very well-trained operators, since interpreting the picture was far from simple, and required the deft use of overlays and predicted radar pictures, and it was never very effective against certain targets, including Berlin. At much the same time as H2S made its debut, the PFF began to receive new, purpose-designed, target markers which burned more brightly and for longer, and which were more difficult for the enemy to 'imitate' if decoy fires were set.

Another view of HR928/'TL-L' of No 35 Sqn, the personal aircraft of the well-known 'Pathfinder Ace', Alec Cranswick, whose family crest is applied below the cockpit. The aircraft has an abbreviated bomb-log on the nose, and is fitted with a nose-mounted 0.303-in 'scare gun' (*Author's Collection*)

With its new equipment, No 35 Sqn went on to play a vital and highly effective role in the attacks against Essen (March 1943), Le Creusot (June 1943) and Peenemünde (August 1943). It was an exceptional unit at the time, with an exceptional succession of pilots and commanders.

The PFF suffered higher-than-average losses (with the exception of the Mosquito force) because of their task, which entailed staying in the target area for longer than the Main Force bombers, and receiving the full weight of the enemy defences before they were degraded by bombing.

There were probably hundreds of examples of self-sacrifice, courage and devotion to duty equal to those which resulted in the award of the Victoria Cross. Some individuals won less prestigious awards, and some went unrecognised altogether, but it would be a pity if all were forgotten.

On 21 December 1943, Graveley-based Halifax pilot Sqn Ldr Julian Sale (OC A Flight, No 35 Sqn) was forced to abort his landing when a 'hung' TI (Target Indicator) burst into flames in the bomb bay. He climbed away and ordered his crew to bail out. His mid-upper gunner's chute pack was burned, however, and Sale returned to Graveley for an emergency landing, ignoring the risk to himself. Both men survived the subsequent crash, although Sale later died of his wounds after being shot down by a Ju 88 in February 1944.

Another legendary figure in No 35 Sqn was Alec Cranswick, who flew a tour with No 214 Sqn on Wellingtons, then volunteered for further service in the Middle East. He had completed 61 sorties by 7 April 1942, when he received the DFC. Cranswick then converted to the Halifax and joined No 419 Sqn, volunteering to transfer to the Pathfinders after five sorties. A complex character, teetotaller Cranswick was educated at St Edwards, Oxford, (the *alma mater* of Douglas Bader, Guy Gibson and Adrian Warburton) and regarded the war as a distasteful, but necessary, evil. He flew a full tour, then returned to No 35 Sqn, which had by then re-equipped with Lancasters, and was subsequently killed.

Wg Cdr Basil Vernon Robinson joined No 35 Sqn in late 1941 after completing a tour on Whitleys. He was one of the pilots involved in the raid on the *Scharnhorst* and *Gneisenau* on 18 December 1941, winning a DFC in the process, and duly taking command of the squadron in March 1942. On the night of 18/19 November 1942, Robinson ordered his crew to bail out when another 'hung' TI caught fire as the aircraft was crossing the Alps after a raid on Turin. Alone in the aircraft, Robinson was astonished to see the fire go out, and he flew back to base solo, with no navigator or flight engineer. Robinson was subsequently promoted to group captain and placed in command of RAF Graveley, but was killed on 23 August 1943 when flying a mission with a No 35 Sqn crew.

The last CO of No 35 Sqn during the unit's Halifax era was Wg Cdr Sydney Patrick 'Pat' Daniels DSO, DFC, who greeted new arrivals on the unit with an axe suspended over his head. Only 23 years old, Daniels was a PFF veteran, having completed previous tours on Whitleys (with No 58 Sqn) and Hampdens (with No 83 Sqn), prior to joining No 35 Sqn. Despite his young age, he proved to be a born leader and was hugely popular with his men, remaining in command as the unit converted to the Lancaster. With the completion of No 35 Sqn's conversion in March 1944, the career of the Halifax in the PFF came to an end.

In the PFF, as in the rest of Bomber Command, the aircrew depended heavily on their hardworking groundcrew, who laboured long and hard, often in poor working conditions, to ensure that the aircraft were in top-notch condition. The Halifax had been designed to fit in peacetime hangars, but with the demands of war, spent most of its life dispersed in the open (*via* Aeroplane)

1

Halifax B II Series I (Special) BB324/ZA-X of No 10 Sqn, Melbourne, April 1943

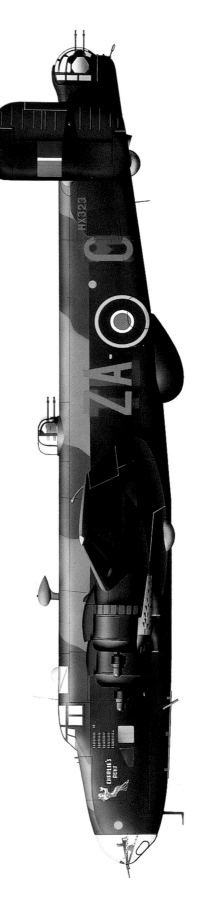

2

Halifax B III HX323/ZA-C of No 10 Sqn, Melbourne, late 1944

3

Halifax B I Series I L9503/TL-P of No 35 Sqn, Linton-on-Ouse, Summer 1941

4

Halifax B II Series I R9441/TL-S of No 35 Sqn, Linton-on-Ouse, Summer 1942

5

Halifax B II Series I W7676/TL-P of No 35 Sqn, Graveley, Summer 1942

6

Halifax B III LW497/MH-W of No 51 Sqn, Snaith, early March 1944

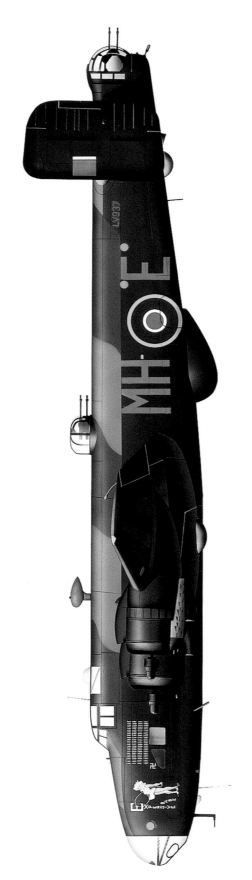

7
Halifax B III LV937/MH-E of No 51 Sqn, Snaith, 25 March 1945

8
Halifax GR II Series IA JP328/BY-H of No 58 Sqn, St Davids, Summer 1944

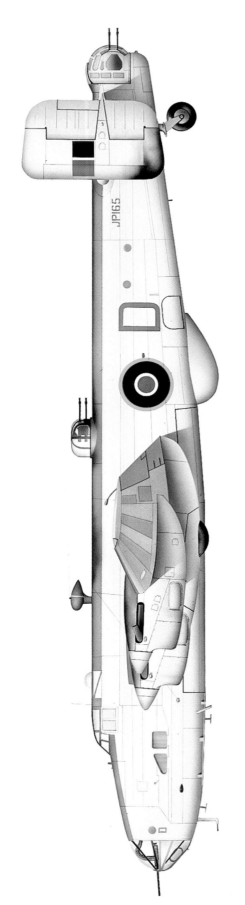

9

Halifax GR II Series IA JP165/D of No 58 Sqn, Stornoway, early 1945

10

Halifax B I Series I L9530/MP-L of No 76 Sqn, Middleton St George, August 1941

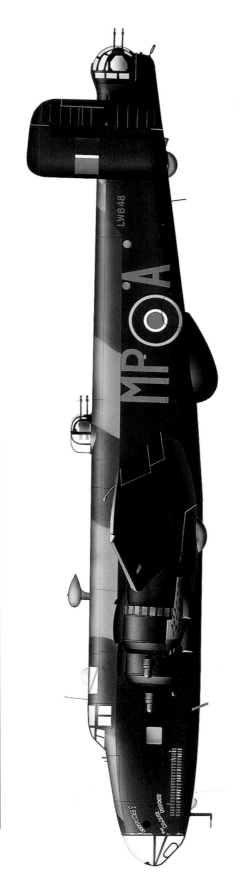

11

Halifax B III LW648/MP-A of No 76 Sqn, Holme-on-Spalding Moor, Autumn 1944

12

Halifax B V Series IA LL126/KN-W of No 77 Sqn, Elvington, Winter 1943

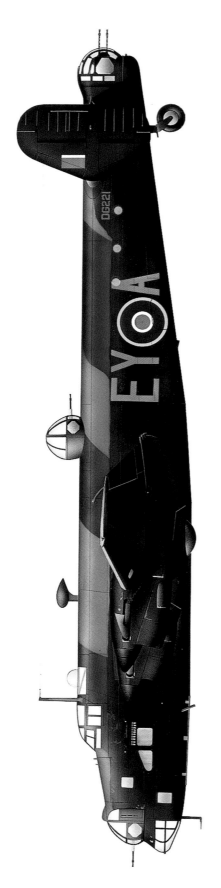

13

Halifax B II Series I DG221/EY-A of No 78 Sqn, Middleton St George, July 1942

14

Halifax B II Series I L9613/NF-V of No 138 (Special Duties) Sqn, detached to Favid, Egypt, December 1942

15
Halifax B V Series I (Special) DG253/NF-F, of No 138 (Special Duties) Sqn, Tempsford, September 1943

16
Halifax B II Series IA JP246/FS-B of No 148 (Special Duties) Sqn, Derna, September 1943

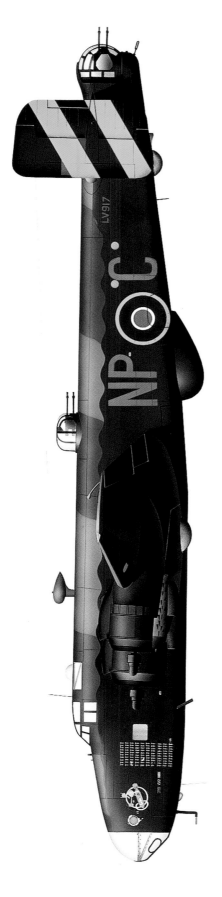

17
Halifax B III LV917/NP-C of No 158 Sqn, Lissett, April 1945

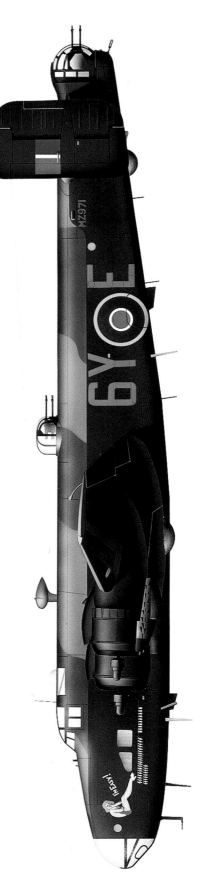

18
Halifax B III (BS) MZ971/6Y-E of No 171 Sqn, North Creake, early 1945

19

Halifax B III (BS) serial unknown/DT-G of No 192 Sqn, Foulsham, late 1944

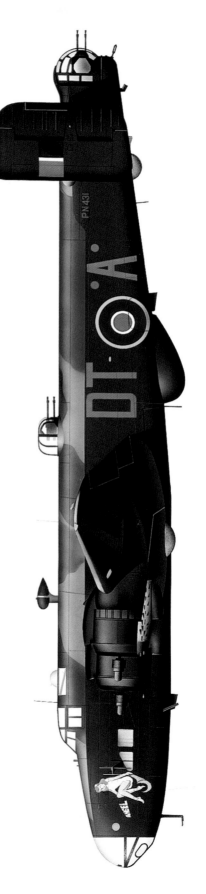

20

Halifax B III (BS) PN431/DT-A of No 192 Sqn, Foulsham, March 1945

21
Halifax A V DG396/QQ, of No 295 Sqn during Operation *Elaborate* (UK–North Africa glider ferry), No 38 Wing, Army Co-operation Command, Holmsley South, June 1943

22
Halifax B III LL573/L8-B of No 347 Sqn, Elvington, Early 1945

23
Halifax B II Series I W7710/LQ·R of No 405 Sqn, RCAF, Topcliffe, Summer 1942

24
Halifax B II Series I (Special) W1173/LQ·X of No 405 Sqn, RCAF, Topcliffe, Summer 1942

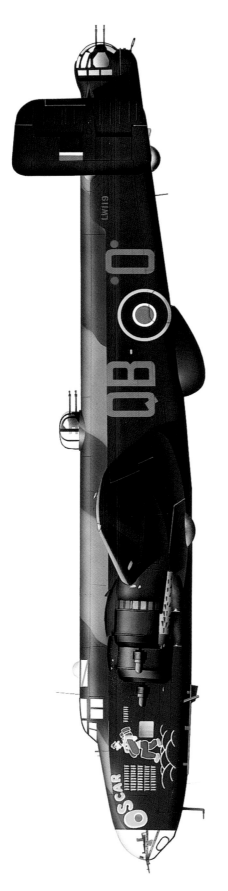

25
Halifax B III LW119/QB-O of No 424 Sqn, RCAF, Topcliffe, November 1944

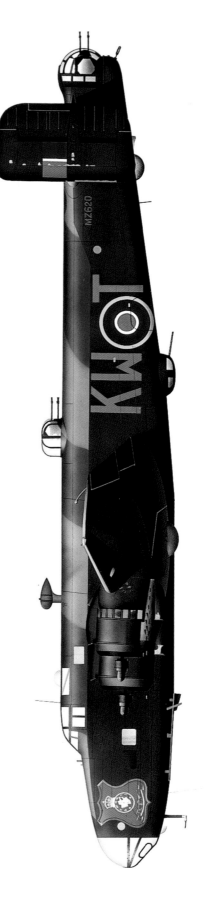

26
Halifax B III MZ620/KW-T of No 425 Sqn, RCAF, Tholthorpe, November 1944

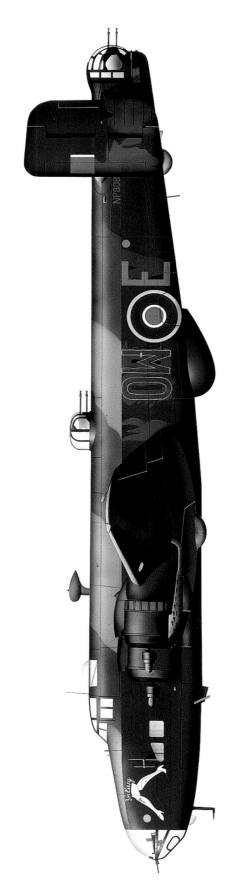

27
Halifax B VII NP808/-E of No 426 Sqn, RCAF, (ex-No 424 Sqn) Linton-on-Ouse, early 1945

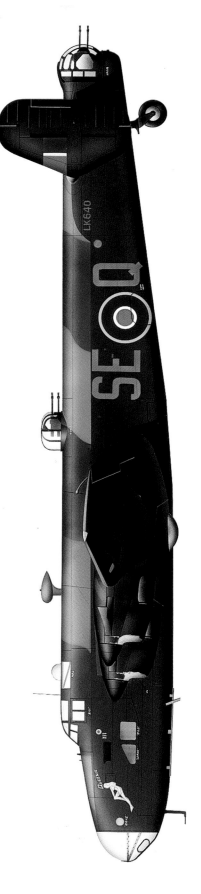

28
Halifax B V Series IA LK640/SE-Q of No 431 Sqn, RCAF, Tholthorpe, Summer 1943

29

Halifax B II Series I W1169/S of No 462 Sqn, RAAF, No 249 Wing, Hosc Raui, September 1943

30

Halifax B III (BS) MZ913/Z5-N of No 462 Sqn, RAAF, Foulsham, April 1945

31
Halifax B III HX266/HD-E of No 466 Sqn, RAAF, Driffield, late 1944

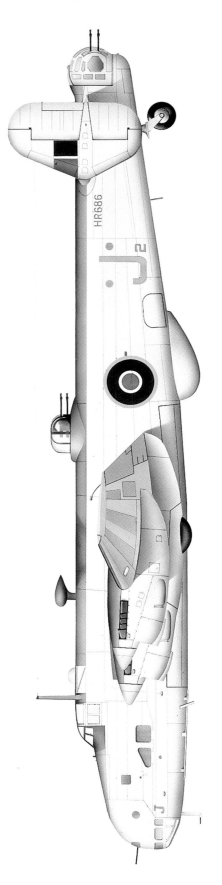

32
Halifax GR II Series I (Special) HR686/J2 of No 502 Sqn, St Eval, Summer 1944

65

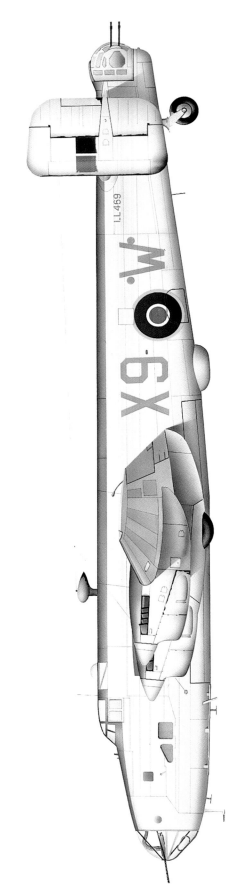

33

Halifax Met V Series IA LL469/X9-W of No 517 Sqn, Brawdy, Spring 1945

34

Halifax Met III LV876/X9-F of No 517 Sqn, Brawdy, Spring 1945

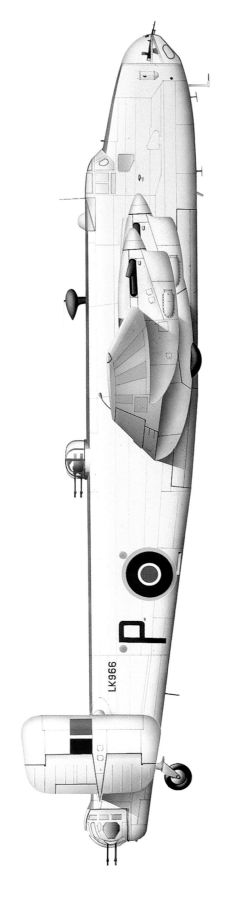

35
Halifax Met V Series IA LK966/P of No 518 Sqn, Stornoway, early 1944

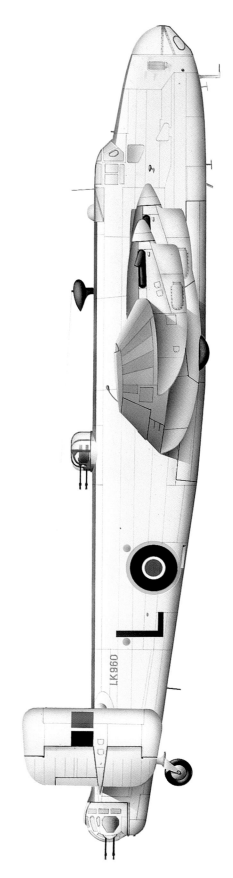

36
Halifax Met V Series IA LK960/2-L of No 520 Sqn, Gibraltar, Summer 1944

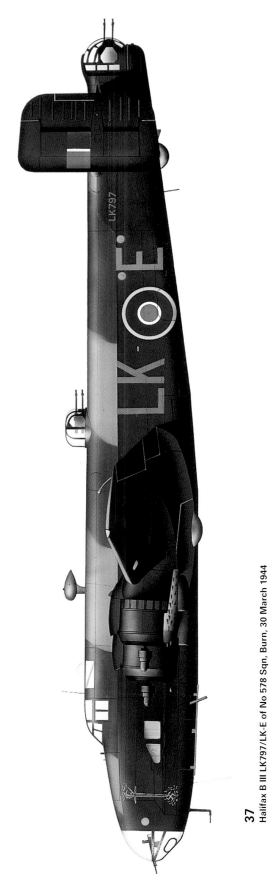

37

Halifax B III LK797/LK-E of No 578 Sqn, Burn, 30 March 1944

38

Halifax A V Series IA (serial unknown)/9U-K of No 644 Sqn, No 38 Group, Tarrant Rushton, D-Day, 6 June 1944

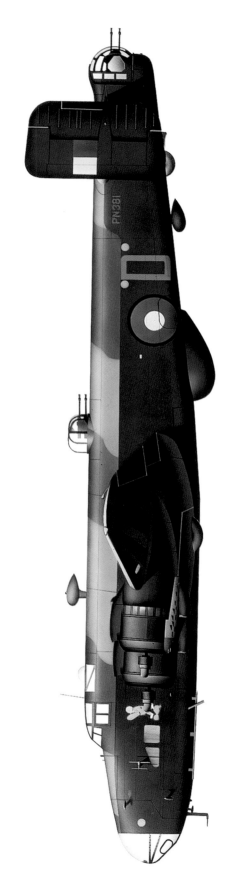

39
Halifax B III (BS) PN381/D of No 1341 Flight, Digri, May 1945

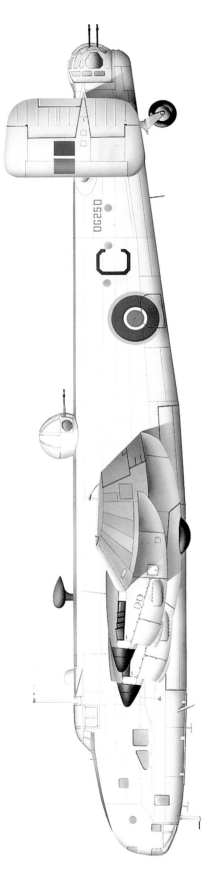

40
Halifax GR V Series I (Special) DG250/C of No 1674 Heavy Conversion Unit, Aldergrove, May 1945

1
Sgt A Stark, RAF, of No 466 Sqn,
RAAF, Driffield, 21 December 1943

2
Flt Sgt C Wilson, RAF, No 466 Sqn,
RAAF, Driffield, 21 December 1943

3
Flt Lt R Kemp, RAF, No 51 Sqn,
Snaith, 7 December 1944

4
Rear gunner from No 466 Sqn,
Driffield, 21 January 1944

5
Flt Lt Ron Hines, RAAF, No 462 Sqn,
RAAF, Foulsham, 1945

6
Mid-fuselage ('Beam') gunner, No 35
Sqn, Linton-on-Ouse, March 1941

SOE HALIFAXES

Modern historical research suggests that Hitler's plans for an invasion of Britain had been abandoned even before the Battle of Britain, and that the troops and invasion barges so prominently 'on-view' in the Channel ports were actually insufficient to be any more than a *ruse de guerre*. Whatever the truth, Germany's failure to eliminate Britain before opening a second front in the east proved to be a fatal mistake. Britain was able to keep German resources diverted in 'side-show theatres' in the Mediterranean and North Africa, thus preventing the Wehrmacht from throwing its full might against the Soviets.

The British Isles became, in effect, an unsinkable aircraft carrier off the coast of Europe, from which 'pinprick' fighter-bomber raids and an escalating strategic bombing campaign were mounted. Britain also became the home of countless 'Governments in exile' from occupied Europe, and became a 'beacon of hope' for people in the occupied countries.

But simply knowing that Britain had not fallen would have brought little advantage to resistance movements in the occupied nations of Europe, nor were propaganda radio broadcasts terribly useful, except in maintaining morale. Fortunately, however, Britain was able to offer more concrete assistance, and set up a massive organisation – the Special Operations Executive (SOE) – whose sole purpose was to support resistance movements with training, supplies, weapons, advice and a degree of co-ordination. Needless to say, running the SOE required extensive use of aircraft, and a number of dedicated units were set up to offer support.

The classic image of SOE aerial operations is the ungainly Westland Lysander landing by dead of night to drop off or pick-up a young agent, but far more significant were the aircraft which never actually landed in hostile territory, but which penetrated covertly to deliver agents or material by parachute. Hudsons (and a few Havocs) were initially used, but both types lacked the range necessary to reach far into occupied Europe.

From October 1941, though, the SOE's Special Duties Squadrons gained a new, more capable type. Three war-weary early mark Halifaxes were specially converted by the Airborne Forces Establishment and began

Seen at Fayid, Egypt, in December 1942, No 138 Sqn's 'V-Victor' was the aircraft used to drop the Heydrich assassination team. The aircraft has a streamlined deflector mast in front of the shrouded tailwheel and a para-dropping hatch in the bottom of the fuselage. An early Handley Page-built B II (the fifth built), L9613 displayed an extremely well-worn appearance by December 1942 (*via Phil Jarrett*)

JP246 was a B II Series IA modified for SOE use and used by No 148 Sqn in the Mediterranean. Seen here undergoing open-air maintenance, it was lost on 8 October 1944 at Brindisi (*via Bruce Robertson*)

operational flying with No 138 Sqn at Newmarket on the night of 7/8 November 1941, with Wg Cdr Rudkowski flying the first mission (Operation *Ruction*) in L6912. Strong headwinds, faulty hydraulics (which allowed the undercarriage to drop) and icing forced Rudkowski to force-land in neutral Sweden on the return journey, but he and his crew were soon repatriated.

Although the Halifaxes were flown primarily by Polish crews, and operated mainly in support of the Polish resistance, they did fly on other tasks. On 28/29 December, for example, Flt Lt Ron Hockey flew three parties (including the team tasked with assassinating Reinhardt Heydrich) to Czechoslovakia. The squadron's Halifax strength increased to five in January 1942, and it moved to Tempsford in March 1942, where it joined No 161 Sqn to form an SOE-dedicated Special Duties (SD) Wing.

Soon after its arrival at Tempsford, No 138 Sqn flew its most unusual mission. On 20 April Wg Cdr Farley and a Polish crew flew a Soviet NKVD team to Austria, but hit a hill on the way to the DZ. Little is known about the circumstances behind this mission, which resulted in the squadron's first loss of a Halifax crew.

Fixated on building up the strength of Bomber Command, Arthur Harris had resented giving up even three war-weary Halifaxes to SOE. Lancasters had yet to arrive, and the Halifax (as the only effective modern 'heavy') was a very precious commodity. Accordingly, No 138 Sqn's Halifaxes flew occasional bombing sorties with No 3 Group whenever they could be spared, and whenever a maximum effort was demanded. This was easier in the summer months, when short, light nights made long-distance supply drops to Eastern Europe prohibitively dangerous.

The Poles, predictably enough, were desperate to hit back at the hated Germans, and on the night of 29/30 October W7774/'T', flown by Flg Off Krol, bomb the Gestapo HQ in Warsaw. They found the target, but abandoned their attack, fearing collateral damage to their long-suffering countrymen. Instead, they bombed Okecie airfield, marking the only raid on a Polish target by an RAF aircraft during the entire war! They were attacked over the North Sea by a pair of Bf 110s, but successfully ditched.

During October 1942, several crews and Halifaxes were attached to No 511 Sqn at Lyneham, flying in the 'straight' transport role running supplies to Libya. The first SOE Halifaxes retained nose and tail turrets, but received a new paratroop hatch, winches for recovering static lines and sheet metal guards and a streamlined deflector mast to stop parachute static lines from fouling the tailwheel.

Halifax sorties flown by the SD units were very different to Main Force or Pathfinder bomber operations. The aircraft inevitably operated alone, almost always below 10,000 ft (no oxygen was carried) and often very much lower. Security was very tight, and usually only the pilot and navigator knew their destination. With the technology of the time, the SOE aircraft were also very vulnerable, since if agents were captured with their radios and code-books, the Germans could 'take- over' the operation, capturing agents as they landed, and downing

the aircraft which brought them. This happened to the first two SOE agents dropped in Holland in November 1942, and led to the loss of 29 No 138 Sqn aircraft over Holland by the end of September 1943.

Unfortunately, the Germans were not the only people eager to take a 'pot-shot' at the SD Halifaxes. The Russians were never more than ambivalent in their attitude to the Poles, and there were suspicions that they sometimes targeted SOE aircraft resupplying the Polish Home Army. In Yugoslavia, there were proven instances of 'blue on blue' engagements. There was bitter rivalry between Tito's communist partisans and the royalists led by Gen Mihailovich, and both sides knew that Halifaxes dropped supplies to either faction on the one mission. Partisans would therefore wait until they had got their delivery and then fire on the departing aircraft, hoping to stop it dropping weapons to the 'enemy'.

Operating alone, often at low level, and sometimes able to route around enemy defences, SOE Halifax crews considered speed and range were more important than defensive firepower (despite the dangers), and a lighter, more streamlined version of the Halifax was hurriedly produced. This, the Halifax B II (SOE), had increased tankage, lower drag engine nacelles and a streamlined metal fairing (the Tempsford, or Z-type, nose) in place of the nose turret. Mid-upper turrets and underwing fuel jettison pipes were removed in order to reduce drag, and the flame-damping exhaust shrouds also vanished, with the exposed exhausts being painted with special heat-resistant paint. Most aircraft had retractable tailwheels, and some had a streamlined 'exit cone' fitted around the paratroop door. A number of B II Series IAs were also modified for SOE use.

No 161 Sqn began converting to the Halifax in December 1942,

Groundcrew pose beside their Halifax at Blida in 1943. No 624 Sqn used the aircraft for SOE support duties, EB147 being a factory-modified B V Series I (Special) (*via Phil Jarrett*)

This No 624 Sqn Halifax B V Series IA (Special) wears a bomb-log on its nose, although the bomb symbols represent agent and supply dropping flights rather than bombing sorties (*via Phil Jarrett*)

operating aircraft from Tempsford and a number of detachments in the Mediterranean and North Africa. The squadron flew from Norway to North Africa, and from France to Poland, although the focus of its activities remained over France. The Halifax also equipped the Polish-manned No 301 (Special Duties) Flight, which became No 1586 (Special Duties) Flight, and was raised to full squadron status in November 1944. This unit focused its activities in supporting the Polish Home Army, but it also assisted resistance groups in Crete, Italy and northern Yugoslavia. Halifax B II Series I (Specials) and Series IAs also equipped two units in North Africa, No 148 Sqn, operating over the Balkans from March 1943, and No 1575 Flight (which became No 624 Sqn in September 1943). The latter unit operated mainly over the south of France, but also over Italy, Corsica, Czechoslovakia, Greece and Yugoslavia.

In October 1943 it was decided that the SOE Halifaxes would be replaced by Stirlings, which were incapable of flying at anything but relatively low altitude, and which were thus useless in Bomber Command's Main Force squadrons. It was planned that the Halifaxes would be converted back to bomber configuration, although feeling against the Halifax within Bomber Command was also beginning to show. From January 1944, the remaining Halifaxes at Tempsford began to be concentrated within No 138 Sqn, with No 148 gradually relying more on the Hudson.

The intensity of operations reached fever-pitch in the run-up to D-Day, and the planned replacement of the Halifax began to slip back. Indeed, it was at this time that the ageing B I Series I (Special) was finally replaced by newer B II derivatives. The inability of the Halifax B V to carry a full bombload led to its rapid re-allocation to other tasks also, and the SOE B IIs were augmented (and in some units replaced) by similarly converted B V Series I (Specials) and Series IAs. This briefly halted the plan to re-equip home-based SOE units with Stirlings, since in the B V they had a Halifax useless to Harris.

In some units the Halifaxes formed the squadron's sole equipment, but in others they operated alongside a variety of types that included Liberators. But in the Mediterranean, No 624 Sqn did convert to the Stirling from July 1944, flying its last Halifax sortie on 13 August.

The Warsaw Rising began on 1 August 1944, when the Polish Home Army seized areas of the city from the Germans. A major Soviet offensive could probably have

One of No 624 Sqn's groundcrew leans against 'his' aeroplane's wheel, waiting for the aircrew to arrive for a night sortie. The aircraft is an SOE-modified B V Series IA Special (*via Phil Jarrett*)

relieved Warsaw, but by sitting back, the Red Army could watch as the Germans and Poles (one new enemy, one old) massacred each other. SOE Halifaxes began flying drops on 4 August, but the aircraft had to fly at very low level to ensure that they reached the right people, and losses were catastrophic. Four No 148 Sqn aircraft were lost on the first night alone.

Air Marshal Slessor refused to permit further flights, but was forced to allow Polish crews to continue from the night of 8/9 August. The operation decimated their ranks and achieved little. for resistance collapsed in late September. Less than half the supplies dropped had reached them.

By the beginning of 1945, the Allied liberation of much of occupied Europe had reduced the requirement for dropping agents and supplies to various resistance movements. Straight transport flights, often by day, had started to dominate from the autumn of 1944, finally allowing some units to re-equip with Stirlings. This was inevitable, not least because replacement Merlin-engined Halifaxes were becoming harder to find.

No 161 Sqn switched the focus of its attentions entirely to Norway and Denmark after September 1944, the squadron phasing out the last of its Halifaxes at much the same time, and beginning to fly an increasing proportion of 'straight' transport flights. No 138 Sqn (the 'father' of SOE units) had discarded its Halifaxes in August 1944, and soon afterwards returned to No 3 Group as a frontline bomber unit. No 624 Sqn disbanded in September 1944, its predominantly French task complete.

After 28 December 1944, the SOE banned further flights in support of the Polish partisans, apparently at the request of advancing Soviet forces. No 301 Sqn was soon sent back to the UK from southern Italy in the spring of 1945 and transferred to transport duties. Only No 148 Sqn continued in the SOE role at 'full tilt', particularly in Italy and the Balkans, although it also occasionally dropped supplies to advancing Soviet forces.

The main focus of No 148 Sqn's ops in early 1945 was in support ofpartisans in northern Italy – which was still occupied by the Germans, and still fighting on the Axis side. But as the year drew on, the unit began dropping agents into Austria and central Czechoslovakia, as well as flying direct support missions for Allied armies as they drove into northern Italy.

No 148 Sqn actually operated right up until the end of the war in Europe, converting to Liberator VIs and the bomber role from 23 May 1945, when its well-worn Halifaxes were finally retired.

Another No 624 Sqn B V Series IA (Special) is pictured waiting for its crew at Blida in 1943. No parachute exit cone is visible, and the aircraft is exceptionally streamlined (*via Phil Jarrett*)

No 100 GROUP

The Halifax lost out to the Lancaster in Bomber Command Main Force squadrons ostensibly because it was slower and lower flying. In fact, as has been seen, the real reasons were more complex, and included the fact that the Halifax was more expensive and more time-consuming to build. The root cause of the Halifax's lower performance lay in the fact that it had been designed to meet a wide requirement, which specified that it should be a multi-role aircraft fitting pre-war hangars, and not as a dedicated European theatre bomber. Thus, the Halifax had a deep and capacious fuselage, with relatively small bomb bays – features which would later allow easy conversion to transport configuration.

The Halifax's roomy interior also meant that it was very well suited to the 'Bomber Support' role – a task which assumed increasing importance as the war progressed, and as new techniques and technology were met by new countermeasures.

Monitoring and analysing radio and radar frequencies, jamming and 'spoofing' all became an integral part of the bitter battle being played out every night in the skies over Germany. The RAF's Elint effort was initially conducted on a small scale, and it was not until 10 December 1940 that the Wireless Intelligence Development Unit reached squadron strength

With miniature kangaroos forming its 'mission tally', Australian pilot Flt Lt Matthews' No 192 Sqn Halifax B III was one of the most colourful in Bomber Command. These ELINT aircraft played a vital role in assessing the equipment and capabilities of Germany's nightfighter arm, and also participated in jamming and deception operations. One *Window*-dropping Halifax could be made to resemble a 50-aircraft raid on enemy radar, and this would raise 150 nightfighters in response, ten of which could be usually relied upon to crash on landing
(*John Crotch via Martin Bowman*)

Jane (actually MZ913, coded Z5-N) was the aircraft of RAAF pilot Flt Lt Ron Hines, subject of one of the figure artworks in this book. The aircraft carries ABC aerial masts below the nose and above the fuselage, and small antenna fairings are visible along the bomb doors (*Jerry Scutts via Martin Bowman*)

An unusual view of a No 192 Sqn Halifax in flight shortly before the end of the war. Named *Angel* and coded 'DT-A', the aircraft carried a comprehensive Elint and jamming antenna fit (*Gp Capt Jack Short via Martin Bowman*)

as No 109 Sqn. The unit subsequently became a Pathfinder Mosquito squadron, leaving behind two flights (Nos 1473 and 1474) in the Elint role.

No 1474 Flight became a squadron in its own right on 4 January 1943, as No 192 Sqn at Feltwell. The unit was equipped with a handful of Mosquitoes and a larger number of Wellington ICs and Xs, and these were intended as interim equipment, pending replacement by Halifaxes. Unfortunately, Arthur Harris was unwilling to see even a handful of his precious 'heavies' diverted from frontline Bomber Command units for what he saw as a 'side-show', and Halifaxes arrived in a trickle, two in January and the next in July. Wellingtons remained in use well into 1944.

No 100 Group was formed on 8 November 1943 in order to co-ordinate the efforts of the RAF's various 'Bomber Support' units. No 192 Sqn moved to Foulsham to join No 100 Group on 25 November, the squadron's Halifaxes being subsequently engaged on both electronic eavesdropping and radar jamming missions, the latter often being flown in direct support of Main Force bomber missions, or as part of diversionary raids. The ECM Halifaxes carried *Mandrel*, which actively jammed German early warning radar, and required six rigid mast antennas along the centreline of the belly. They also used *Window* and even dropped bombs from the Halifax's inner wing bomb-bays.

The unit soon demonstrated its usefulness to the bomber campaign, and began receiving Hercules-engined B IIIs in January 1944 at much the same time as the variant was passed to the first frontline bomber squadrons.

Another Bomber Support unit in the form of No 199 Sqn transferred to No 100 Group and North Creake on 1 May 1944, where it initially operated Stirlings. These were never viewed as being anything other than interim operational equipment, since the decision had already been taken that No 100 Group would standardise on the Halifax – the squadron re-equipped with Halifaxes in February 1945. No 171 Sqn joined No 100 Group's order of battle on 8 September 1944, forming at North Creake from C Flight of No 199 Sqn, and quickly re-equipping with Halifaxes. The new squadrons tended to perform *Mandrel* and *Window* operations, leaving the more specialised task of signals investigation and communications jamming to No 192 Sqn (which continued to fly *Window* and RCM missions as well).

Many Foulsham-based Halifaxes wore stylish (though often slightly risqué) nose-art. *SLEEPY Gal* decorated the nose of a No 192 Sqn Halifax during early 1945 (*Gp Capt Jack Short via Martin Bowman*)

The final Halifax unit to transfer to No 100 Group was the Australian-manned No 462 Sqn, which switched from No 4 Group in December 1944. The unit moved from Driffield to Foulsham and re-equipped with Halifaxes modified to carry the new *Airborne Cigar* radar jamming equipment, with two prominent mast antennas above the fuselage and another below. Some aircraft were also fitted with the American *Piperack* system, which was a derivative of *Mandrel* covering the 60-93 MHz range (the bands in which the FuG 220 *Liechtenstein* radar, carried by many German nightfighters, operated).

Typically, *Window*-carrying Halifaxes would feint away from the Main Force to draw fighters away from the real target, and into the patrol areas of friendly Mosquitoes, before withdrawing behind the *Mandrel* screen. Meanwhile, *Airborne Cigar* would be used to screen the Main Force bombers from enemy radar.

As the German defences crumbled, No 100 Group's operations increased in tempo, with the Halifaxes flying 'spoof' raids to further over-stretch the disintegrating German nightfighter arm. Sometimes, the number of Bomber Support aircraft sent out was greater than the number of heavy bombers. For example, on the night of 22/23 February 1945, 35 Lancasters attacked railway viaducts, 86 Mosquitoes went to Berlin, Bremen and Efurt and 23 Mosquito nightfighters went out on patrol. These aircraft were supported by no less than 43 Bomber Support platforms, most of them Halifaxes!

The Halifax also played a part in electronic warfare missions in the Far East, No 1341 Flight forming at Digri in May 1945, and operating in the Elint role until the end of hostilities, when it transferred to transport operations.

Halifaxes continued in use for Bomber Support operations after the war, primarily with the newly-formed Radio Warfare Establishment at Watton. This unit formed from the nucleus left by No 192 Sqn when it disbanded. The last Halifaxes were struck off charge in February 1947.

AIRBORNE FORCES AND TRANSPORT

T he mass use of paratroops proved to be such a success during Hitler's *Blitzkrieg* of 1940 that it prompted the rapid development of a similar capability in Britain, where ancient Whitleys were pressed into service for paratroop dropping and glider-towing. The Whitley served the Airborne Forces well in both roles, despite its age and poor performance, but it soon became clear that a replacement was needed – not least to tow the huge new Hamilcar tank-carrying glider.

In October 1941 (the very month that SOE received its first agent-dropping Halifaxes) the Airborne Forces Development Unit at Ringway also received its first Halifax, R9435, which was modified with a similar circular paratroop hatch. The unit quickly developed the streamlined exit cone, static line retrieval winch and glider towing hook that were eventually fitted to all Airborne Forces Halifaxes. Five Halifaxes were on charge by December 1941, and these were soon heavily engaged in trials with the new Horsa and Hamilcar gliders.

The Halifax made its operational debut as a glider tug on 17 November 1942 when two No 38 Wing aircraft towed two Horsa gliders to Norway for a Commando attack on facilities producing deuterium oxide ('Heavy Water') for the Nazi atomic bomb programme. The first Horsa crashed on landing, killing eight of its 16 Royal Engineer occupants and injuring four more. The latter were executed by a German doctor at the scene, and the remainder captured and executed at a later date. The second Horsa, and its occupants, met a similar fate (four Commandos were poisoned in hospital by the Gestapo), while the Halifax crashed into a ridge soon after releasing the glider. The 'Heavy Water' plant was subsequently successfully attacked by resistance and SOE personnel.

Halifaxes began to replace the

The heavyweight Hamilcar could be towed aloft by a single Halifax, but as this sequence shows, tests were also conducted using a pair of tugs, one of which would return to base after take-off (*via Dr Alfred Price*)

The A V was essentially a B V Series
IA with a glider towing hook behind
the tailwheel and a paratroop hatch
in the lower fuselage
(*via Phil Jarrett*)

Whitleys of No 38 Wing, Army Co-operation Command, in February 1943, first with No 295 Sqn. This unit flew glider towing, leaflet-dropping and even 'straight' bombing sorties, completing a number of operations, including an attack on a French transformer station at Distre on 19/20 February. The unit soon had another task – ferrying empty Horsas to North Africa for use in the Sicilian invasion in May/June 1943.

Most went via Portreath to Salé, in Morocco, with Coastal Command navigators attached to the unit to ensure accurate navigation on the long and arduous over-water flight. There were a number of incidents, with Horsas being forced to cast off and ditch, most notably on 14 June, when a Halifax/Horsa combination was attacked by two Focke-Wulf Fw 200 Condors. The glider cast off and ditched, and the Halifax was shot down.

Seven Horsa-towing Halifaxes participated in the initial assault on Sicily on 9/10 July (Operation *Ladbroke*), and five more in Operation *Fustian* on 13/14 July, which was the last airborne assault of the campaign. One Halifax was shot down by flak on the latter operation, but several of the gliders reached their targets. Under Operation *Elaborate*, No 295 Sqn continued ferrying gliders to North Africa. On 17 September, one combination was attacked by about eight Ju 88s. The glider pilot unselfishly cast off, and the Halifax (piloted by Flg Off Norman) then successfully evaded the Ju 88s, sustaining major damage but making it to its destination. The Halifax left behind one Ju 88 in the water, downed by Sgt Grant – the rear gunner subsequently won a DFM for his kill.

The last combination left for Salé on 23 September, and in October No 295 Sqn began conversion to the Albemarle. Ten of its Halifax crews were posted to form the nucleus of the new No 298 Sqn's A Flight, with 12 from No 297 forming B Flight. The new unit formed at Tarrant Rushton with 17 Halifax A Vs (and seven Horsas) on 4 November. By this time No 38 Wing had become No 38 Group, with the single Halifax squadron augmented by four squadrons of Stirlings and four more of Albemarles.

Training with the massive Hamilcar began later that month, and the squadron also trialled freight panniers and the carriage of jeeps and 75 mm guns slung in the former bomb-bay. The Halifax crews also got used to dropping larger and larger sticks of paratroops (reaching 30 in number), all in preparation for the invasion of mainland Europe.

No 298 Sqn grew larger and larger, until on 16 March 1944 the unit's C Flight split off to form the nucleus of No 644 Sqn – each unit had an establishment of 18 Halifaxes (plus two spares). The aircraft were retro-fitted with *Gee* and *Rebecca* Mk II to allow more accurate navigation, and the early trouble-prone Merlin XX engines were replaced by more reliable Merlin 22s, although the re-engining proceeded slowly, with only 23 aircraft powered by the new powerplant by the end of March 1944. Only Merlin 22 engined aircraft were cleared to tow the corpulent Hamilcar.

On the eve of Operation *Overlord*, six Halifaxes towed Horsas which captured the bridges over the Orne river and the Caen canal, and then made a diversionary bombing attack on a cement works at Caen. On D-Day itself, each of the two Halifax units towed 15 Horsas and a pair of Hamilcars across the Channel in the morning. One Halifax was shot down, but its No 298 Sqn crew were recovered. Later that day, the units participated in Operation *Mallard*, each towing 15 Hamilcars and a single Horsa to reinforce the Airborne troops already in France. No 298 Sqn lost another Halifax, but the crew successfully ditched in the Channel.

Between 10 and 27 June, the Halifaxes of No 38 Group flew an intensive shuttle of resupply flights, sometimes dropping cargo by parachute, sometimes towing supply-laden gliders. On one occasion, a Halifax even towed a Hamilcar stuffed with Spitfire mainplanes to a beachhead airstrip. The squadrons continued to fly resupply missions throughout the late summer and autumn, but were also heavily committed to supporting SAS and SOE groups operating behind enemy lines.

The Halifaxes played a major part in the ill-fated operation (*Market*

A Merlin 22-engined Halifax A V (with four-bladed props) snarls along with a GAL Hamilcar floating serenely behind. Both aircraft are bedecked with D-Day stripes (*via* Aeroplane)

Tarrant Rushton seen during the D-Day afternoon, with the Halifaxes of Nos 298 and 644 Sqns lined up flanking the runway, on which are arrayed two Horsas and 30 Hamilcars. More gliders are dispersed elsewhere on the field. A handful of the Halifaxes still have three-bladed propellers, but they are already a rarity (*via* Aeroplane)

More Halifax A 5s seen at Tarrant Rushton on D-Day. '9U' codes belong to No 644 Sqn, and '8T' to No 298 Sqn. All the aircraft have nose-mounted 'scare guns' (*via* Aeroplane)

Garden) intended to seize and hold the bridge over the Rhine at Arnhem, in Holland. A well-publicised failure, the Arnhem operation nevertheless saw the transport of 4500 men, 95 guns and 544 Jeeps by glider to a point 60 miles behind the enemy frontline. No Halifaxes were lost during the operation, although many were hit by flak.

The two No 38 Group Halifax units had by then started re-equipping with Hercules-powered A IIIs and A VIIs, thus allowing the Albemarle-equipped Nos 296 and 297 Sqns to re-equip with their surplus A Vs. These units used Merlin-powered A Vs until February 1945, when they re-equipped with A IIIs. By the time of Operation *Varsity*, Nos 298 and 644 Sqns at Woodbridge and Nos 296 and 297 Sqns at Earl's Colne operated A IIIs – No 298 Sqn could also boast seven new A VIIs. This combined force was used to tow 72 Horsas and 48 Hamilcars (mainly towed by No 644 Sqn) transporting members of the US 6th Airborne Division to the landing zones near Wesel. Five Halifaxes were lost to flak, but the operation was a great success, as were subsequent re-supply missions.

Immediately following the German surrenders in both Denmark and Norway, Halifaxes (including the last few A Vs still in use) were used to fly in British troops to oversee the transition back to local control (Operations *Schnapps* and *Doomsday*, respectively). The Halifax was destined to remain the workhorse of the Airborne Forces, continuing to serve until

replaced by the Hastings in 1948. There was even a new, improved Airborne Forces variant, the A IX, but postwar use of the aircraft lies outside the scope of this book.

FAR EAST SERVICE

In October 1944, two Halifax A IIIs had been deployed to India for trials

in the Far East Airborne Forces role, and they proved to be remarkably successful despite the very high temperatures encountered. Interestingly, the Halifaxes held up better than the gliders they towed, whose wooden airframes shrank, distorted or cracked in the heat. The aircraft served with No 1577 Flight, which had previously evaluated the Lancaster and Halifax B V in Indian conditions, finding the Merlin-powered Halifax to be far superior, although 'over-finned' and with a tendency to 'weathercock' due to it big rectangular vertical surfaces. Following the glider-towing trials, No 1577 Flight continued to operate in the Airborne Forces role, primarily towing heavily-laden Hamilcars throughout India.

With the end of hostilities in Europe, 24 tropicalised Halifax A VIIs of No 298 Sqn (all fitted with the early, flush-fitting, 3000-lb ventral freight panniers) were flown out to Raipur in July 1945, having originally been intended to form part of Tiger Force for the planned assault on Japan. Fortunately, the need for this was removed by the dropping of atomic bombs on Hiroshima and Nagasaki, which prompted an immediate Japanese surrender, saving thousands (and quite probably millions) of lives. The Halifaxes were re-fitted with the bigger 8000-lb panniers soon after arriving in India. From September, the squadron transferred from the Airborne Forces role to more general transport duties.

The undertaking of straightforward transportation flights was by no means new to the Halifax. Four time-expired B IIs had been locally converted as freighters at No 144 MU, Maison Blanche, for transport duties in North Africa, where they proved to be especially useful for carrying outsized loads (aero engines and fighter fuselages) in the former bomb-bay. Subsequently, a more sophisticated transport version was created in the UK through the conversion of surplus B III bombers into C III configuration.

The first of these aircraft equipped C Flight of No 246 Sqn, before being handed over to No 187 Sqn at Merryfield in March 1945. The type also went to No 96 Sqn at Leconfield, before both units began conversion to Dakotas in March/April 1945. The transport Halifax C VI and C VIII would continue to see service with the postwar RAF.

This No 644 Sqn A V bears signs of intensive use in support of the D-Day landings. The aircraft has a mission tally consisting of the Airborne Forces' Pegasus insignia in miniature (*via Phil Jarrett*)

The final wartime Airborne Halifax was the A VII, shown here. The aircraft was basically an 'Airborne' conversion of the B VII bomber (*Author's Collection*)

COASTAL COMMAND

It has been famously claimed that a single four-engined bomber diverted to Coastal Command did 20 times as much damage to Germany's economy and war machine than it would have done remaining employed on Main Force bombing missions. This view is probably accurate, and has come to be widely accepted, but that was far from the case at the time. As with other non-Bomber Command outfits, Coastal Command initially struggled to get hold of Halifaxes due to 'Bomber' Harris's resentment of what he saw as peripheral 'side-shows'.

But as the war drew on, the usefulness of Coastal Command in fighting the U-boats and ensuring the safety of the convoys became steadily more apparent. The anti-U-boat war was fought far out in the Atlantic and from the Norwegian Coast to south of the Bay of Biscay, resulting in the Command's limited force being greatly over-stretched.

Therefore, from October 1942 Bomber Command Halifax and Lancaster units were temporarily attached to Coastal Command. The first of these detachments, to Beaulieu, were made by Nos 158 (with five Halifaxes) and 405 Sqns (with 15). No 158 Sqn returned to Bomber Command in December, but No 405 remained until March 1943, attacking several U-boats and a number of French harbours during its tour of duty.

These temporary tours marked only a beginning. In the face of disapproval and hostility from Harris, the Command gained two of its own Halifax units, with Nos 58 and No 502 Sqns trading in their ancient Whitleys for Halifax B IIs in December 1942 and January 1943, respectively. The aircraft were fitted with ASV III search radar from February, as well as the primitive radar warning receiver, *Boozer*. With full Coastal Command modifications, the aircraft became GR IIs.

Armed with six 250-lb depth charges, and fitted with additional fuel tanks in the bomb-bay, Halifaxes flew long-range ASW patrols – especially over the Bay of Biscay, where they were often met by German long-range fighters. January 1943 saw the issue of an order which dictated that all Coastal Command Halifaxes would be painted white with extra dark sea grey topsides, but this order took some time to be implemented.

No 502 Sqn scored the first submarine kill credited to the Halifax on 29 March 1943, but the successful crew was forced to bail out upon returning to England when unbroken cloud prevented them from finding their base (at St Eval, on the north Cornish coast), or a suitable diversion! No 58 Sqn opened its score on 7 May 1943 by

Four-bladed propellers identify this aircraft as a GR II for Coastal Command, despite the standard Bomber Command camouflage. Neither ASV radar nor a Preston-Green ventral gun turret are fitted (*Author's collection*)

Halifax Met V Series IA LK966 was issued to No 518 Sqn in January 1944, and is seen here flying near its Tiree base. The aircraft had an exceptionally high demarcation between its extra dark sea grey topsides and its white undersurfaces. (*via Phil Jarrett*)

sinking U-663. This proved to be the first of three such kills for the unit that month, with U-528 following four days later and U-463 on 15 May. On 16 May, another No 58 Sqn Halifax sank the Italian submarine *Tazzoli*. Finally, on the last day of the month the unit shared in the destruction of U-563, which was eventually finished off by a second No 58 Sqn Halifax and Sunderlands from Nos 10 and 228 Sqns.

The Halifax was a relatively easy target for enemy fighters, although it sometimes proved able to defend itself. In early April 1943, for example, a No 58 Sqn aircraft fought off seven Ju 88s for 47 minutes, scoring hits on three of the enemy aircraft before they broke off the engagement. The Halifax returned to base with one bullet hole through the tailplane and three small dents on a turret fairing. In the interests of increasing the defensive armament of the Halifax, the aircraft was fitted with a nose-mounted 0.50-in machine gun from mid-1943, this proving particularly useful for suppressing AAA from surfaced U-boats.

Tactics were also refined throughout the war, with some four-aircraft formations being flown, and with extensive trials leading to an endurance of 13 hours being set as the maximum, although at least one 18-hour patrol was flown by the Coastal Command Development Unit. Trials were also conducted with rocket projectiles, and although successful, these were not adopted by frontline Halifax units.

On 5 December 1943, Nos 58 and 502 Sqns moved to St Davids, on the Welsh coast, where they formed a Halifax Wing with the first Halifax-equipped Meteorological unit at the nearby satellite airfield at Brawdy.

Operations continued much as before until August 1944, with anti-submarine patrols, anti-shipping strikes and armed reconnaissance sorties. Targets then began to dry up in French waters, and the two squadrons were re-deployed to Stornoway, in the Outer Hebrides. From October, the squadrons concentrated on night anti-shipping strikes in the Kattegat and the Skaggerak, interdicting German shipping between Germany, Denmark and Norway with some degree of success. Targets were located using ASV, before flare-lit attacks were made using the proven combination of 600-lb bombs and the Mk XIV bombsight.

Increased German nightfighter activity forced Halifaxes to operate at lower altitudes (200 ft was the optimum height), and this proved to be effective, since fighters rarely pressed home attacks at such heights. Only nine Halifaxes failed to return from patrols during the year, although accidents accounted for several more, and there were many 'close scrapes'.

Nos 58 and 502 Sqns finally replaced their Merlin-engined Halifaxes with Hercules-powered GR IIIs in February and March 1945, and these continued to fly intensively, primarily in the anti-shipping role. March saw an all-time record of 101 attacks (resulting in the sinking of an estimated 5998 tons) and the loss of four aircraft. Successes and losses continued at this frightening tempo until May. Both units sunk their last vessels on 3 May, and were disbanded together on the 25th of that same month.

METEOROLOGICAL HALIFAX

Accurate weather forecasting had a vital role to play in the planning of all operations, and the collection of reliable data necessitated flying long-range sorties far out over the ocean. The aircraft obtained carefully calibrated barometric pressure, temperature and humidity readings, and made records of weather, cloud and wind direction and strength. The role was initially assigned to Hampdens, but these were short-ranged, small, cramped and vulnerable, and No 518 Sqn re-equipped with specially-modified Halifaxes at Stornoway in July 1943, moving to Tiree (an island base off the west coast of Scotland) in September. No 517 Sqn re-equipped with converted Halifax B Vs (known as Met Vs) in August 1943, at St Eval, and duly became the first Meteorological Halifax squadron to fly operational sorties.

Met Vs were converted by Cunliffe-Owen to operate *Gee* and/or *Loran* for accurate navigation, and were also fitted with precision radio altimeters and a psychrometer to measure temperature and humidity. Some aircraft featured a B3 drift meter, whilst others utilised ASV II radar.

Use of the Halifax allowed the employment of specialist Meteorological Observers, freeing navigators for the already challenging task of accurate navigation over water. No 517 Sqn flew a triangular 'Epicure B' route from Brawdy, timed for the terminal point to be reached at midday and again at midnight, while No 518 Sqn flew 'straight-out-and-return' flights, known as a 'Mercer' on a track of 265°T out to 700 nm from base.

The third Halifax Met squadron, No 520 at Gibraltar, flew a similar 'out-and-back' profile known as 'Nocturnal'. On these sorties, the aircraft performed a series of step-climbs and descents to particular pressure levels, and took sea level readings every 100 nm. At the end of the leg, it made a circular climb to 22,000 ft. Meteorological data was encoded and sent back in five five-figure groups. No 518 Sqn later (from February 1944) received an additional commitment to fly a triangular 'Bismuth' (270°T for 550 nm, 045°T for 400 nm, then home!) with the apex near Iceland.

The Halifax Met squadrons took great pride in fulfilling their commitments whatever the weather. During 1944, for example, No 518 Sqn lost only two days flying, and then only after attempting to get airborne. Only one aircraft may have been lost to enemy action, but many more fell victim to accidents or to the weather. At the end of the day, the Merlin engine was not suited to the role, which involved a long, high-boost, low rev 'slog' for maximum range, followed by a rapid climb. Returning on three engines was common.

The Halifax would have a role to play in Coastal Command in the Meteorological role for some years after the war, but that, as they say, is another story.

Another view of LK966, this time pictured at its Tiree base after the airborne photograph was taken. No 518 Sqn moved to Northern Ireland shortly before the end of the war, although this aircraft had transferred to No 520 Sqn, in Gibraltar, and been lost (on 24 November 1944) by then (*via Phil Jarrett*)

This Halifax Met V wears the 'X9-' codes of No 517 Sqn, but is seen here in the Halifax graveyard at Rawcliffe immediately after the war. Unusually for a Meteorological aircraft, it has a Preston-Green turret below the fuselage (*via Phil Jarrett*)

THE END

T he Halifax was already in decline as the war drew to a close, with a gradual standardisation on the Lancaster taking place within Bomber Command. The decision to replace the Halifax had been taken many years before, and was based on the combat record of the original Merlin-engined versions. It certainly took no account whatsoever of the improved performance of the Hercules-engined Halifax, or of the greater versatility and adaptability of the Handley Page aeroplane.

Thus, by VE-Day, No 6 Group (which had been comprised solely of 14 Halifax units on 1 January) had been reduced to five wholly Halifax-equipped squadrons. Another operated 21 Halifaxes and one Lancaster (the first of many!), while four more squadrons were fully equipped with Lancasters, but still retained some Halifaxes pending disposal, and four more units had only Lancasters on charge. In short, No 6 Group was well on the way to being 'all-Lancaster'. There can be little doubt that No 4 Group would have followed suit had the war lasted longer.

The insatiable appetite of Bomber Command's frontline squadrons for Lancasters ensured that No 100 Group, Coastal Command and the Airborne Forces continued to rely on the Halifax, which remained in production. In fact, the aircraft's capacious and comfortable fuselage, and excellent long-range performance, made it the preferred choice for the ECM, Elint, ASV, Meteorological and airborne roles, and the aircraft was far from second-best. But once the war was over, there were huge numbers of surplus Lancasters and rather fewer Halifaxes, and there was great pressure on all Commands to standardise on the Lancaster, pending the introduction of the Lincoln and Shackleton, and the first jet bombers.

Although there was little argument that the Halifax was a better maritime patrol aircraft than the Lancaster, there was considerable logic for the Lancaster to be adopted in its stead once the war was over. The Lancaster was retained in the bomber and survey roles, while the related York formed the backbone of Transport Command, and the Lincoln was selected as Bomber Command's chosen interim bomber. In these circumstances, many felt that to retain another aircraft type for Coastal Command, even if it were marginally superior, made little sense. Remarkably, though, Halifaxes did remain in service in Coastal Command, albeit

Underwing serial numbers reappeared soon after the end of the war, as seen on this B VI. The Halifax bomber itself disappeared from the scene very rapidly, although the type remained in Coastal Command service and in the Airborne Forces role for some years (*via Phil Jarrett*)

The Halifax also enjoyed a brief postwar career in civil markings. This is one of BOAC's Haltons – other Halifaxes served with smaller operators, most notably during the Berlin Airlift

in diminishing numbers, and only in the Meteorological reconnaissance role. The last Coastal Command Halifax, Met 6 RG841, made its final operational flight (from Gibraltar to No 48 MU at Hawarden) as late as 17 March 1952.

The advantages of the Halifax in the airborne role, and in 'hot and high' conditions, were even more conclusive. When No 617 Sqn's Lancasters and No 298 Sqn's Halifaxes operated side-by-side in India, it was found that the fomer were so prone to over-heating that they had to get take-off clearance prior to starting up, and had to be parked near the runway – Halifaxes had no such poblems.

The A VII and A IX were thus retained until the introduction of the Hastings, and the last examples did not disappear from the frontline until October 1948. Civil-registered Halifaxes also played a part in the Berlin Airlift, while small numbers of RAF aircraft served with Airborne Forces development, training and test units until 1954. Coincidentally, this was also the year that the Pakistani air force retired the last of its Halifax bombers, although a handful may have lingered on in Egyptian service.

It is interesting to speculate on what might have happened to the Halifax had the atomic bombs not been dropped. Tiger Force (the force set up for the end of the war in the Pacific) was to have used Lancasters, but the clear superiority of the Halifax in hot conditions could easily have forced, or prompted, a change. But it was not to be, and no Halifaxes survived in service long enough for anyone to realise that it would be good to save one for posterity. By contrast, the French Navy and RCAF retained Lancasters into the 1960s, ensuring that some were saved for museums.

Fortunately, two Halifaxes have been recovered from lakes in Norway for museum display, one of which resides in unrestored condition in the RAF Museum at Hendon. The second aircraft is presently being painstakingly restored for the RCAF Memorial Museum at Trenton. Finally, a third 'Halifax' forms the centrepiece of the Yorkshire Air Museum at Elvington, this aircraft being comprised of portions of several different crashed Halifaxes, together with newly-built sections and the modified wing of a Handley Page Hastings.

For many years it was supposed that the Halifax had disappeared without trace. Then, in July 1973, No 35 Sqn's W1048/'TL-S' was recovered from a Norwegian Lake for display in the RAF Museum. Another Norwegian Lake gave up a later Halifax, which is now being restored for display in Canada, and a third Halifax has been created from various parts salvaged from crashed aircraft, a Hastings wing and new-built components (*via Phil Jarrett*)

APPENDICES

APPENDIX A

HALIFAX UNITS

The RAF's frontline Halifax units are listed below, with formation date, assignment, dates of receiving new variants (and dates to which those variants served), together with movements and fates. Postwar histories are not detailed, and postwar and training/second-line units are listed without movement and variant details

No 10 Sqn ('SHINY TEN')
12/41, No 4 Gp bomb sqn with B I (8/42) and B II (3/44) at Leeming (ex-Whitley). 7/42-9/42 det to Aqir, 8/42 to Melbourne. 3/44 B III (5/45). To Transport Command 7/5/45. Codes ZA-

No 35 ('MADRAS PRESIDENCY') SQN
11/40, No 4 Gp bomb sqn with B I (2/42) at Boscombe Down. 11/40 to Leeming, 12/40 to Linton-on-Ouse. 10/41 B II (1/44). 8/42 No 8 (PFF) Gp, Graveley. 10/42 B III (3/44). 3/44 Lancaster. Codes TL-

No 47 SQN
9/46, postwar Transport Command Squadron formed through re-numbering of No 644 Sqn. Re-equipped with Hastings 10/48. Codes MOHD-

No 51 SQN
11/42, No 4 Gp bomb sqn with B II (1/44) at Snaith (ex-Whitley). 1/44 B III (5/45). To Transport Command 7/5/45. Codes MH-, LK- (C Flt) and C6- (C Flt)

No 58 SQN
12/42, No 19 Gp ASV sqn with GR II (3/45). 3/43 to St Eval (No 19 Gp), 6/43 to Holmsley South, 12/43 to St Davids, 9/44 to Stornoway (No 18 Gp). 3/45 GR III. Disbanded 25/5/45. Codes BY-

No 76 SQN
5/41, No 4 Gp bomb sqn with B I (3/42) at Linton (ex-C Flt, No 35 Sqn). 6/41 to Middleton St George. 10/41 B II (3/43). MEAF det absorbed by No 462 Sqn, 9/42. 9/42 to Linton-on-Ouse. 2/43 B V (2/44). 6/43 to Holme on

Spalding Moor. 1/44 B III (4/45), 3/45 B VI (5/45). To Transport Command 7/5/45. Codes MP-

No 77 SQN
10/42, No 4 Gp bomb sqn with B II (6/44) at Elvington (ex-Whitley). 4/44 B V (5/44). 5/44 to Full Sutton, B III (3/45). 3/45 B VI (8/45). To Transport Command 7/5/45. Codes KN-

No 78 SQN
3/42, No 4 Gp bomb sqn with B II (1/44) at Croft (ex-Whitley). 6/42 to Middleton St George, 9/42 to Linton-on-Ouse, 6/43 to Breighton. 1/44 B III (4/45), 4/45 B VI (7/45). To Transport Command 7/5/45. Codes EY-

No 96 SQN
12/44, Transport Command sqn with C III (4/45) at Leconfield. 3/45 to Cairo West. 4/45 Dakota. Codes 6H-

No 102 ('CEYLON') SQN
12/41, No 4 Gp bomb sqn with B II (3/44) at Dalton (ex-Whitley). 6/42 to Topcliffe, 8/42 to Pocklington. 3/44 B III (2/45). 2/45 B VI (9/45). To Transport Command 7/5/45. Codes DY-

No 103 SQN
7/42, No 1 Gp bomb sqn with B II (10/42) at Elsham Wolds. 10/42 Lancaster. Codes PM-

No 113 SQN
9/46, postwar Transport Command Squadron formed through re-numbering of No 620 Sqn. Disbanded 5/47. Codes MOHC-

No 138 SQN
8/41, No 3 Gp mixed Special Duties sqn, added B IIs (8/44) at Newmarket. 12/41 to Stradishall, 3/42 to Tempsford. 1/43 B V (8/44). 8/44 Stirling IV. Codes NF-

No 148 SQN
3/43, Mediterranean Air Command mixed Special Duties sqn, added B II (5/45) at Gambut. 4/43 to Derna, 9/43 to Tocra, 1/44 to Brindisi. 7/44 B V (5/45). Postwar standardised on Liberator. Codes FS-

No 158 SQN

6/42, No 4 Gp bomb sqn with B II (12/43) at East Moor (ex-Wellington). 11/42 to Rufforth, 2/43 to Lissett. 12/43 B III (5/45). 4/45 B VI (5/45). To Transport Command 7/5/45. Codes NP-

No 161 SQN

9/42, No 3 Gp Special Duties sqn, added B IIs (12/42) at Tempsford. 10/42 B V (10/44). 10/44 continued with Hudson and Stirling IV. Codes MA-

No 171 SQN

10/44, No 100 Gp ECM sqn, added B III (BS) (7/45) at North Creake. Disbanded 7/45. Codes 6Y- and EX-

No 178 SQN

5/43, Mediterranean Air Command bomb sqn, added B IIs (to Liberator II) at Hosc Raui (Ghemines). 9/43 replaced Halifaxes with Liberator III. Codes unknown

No 187 SQN

2/45, Transport Command sqn with C III (from Halifax Flt, No 246 Sqn) at Merryfield. 3/45 Dakota. Codes unknown

No 190 SQN

5/45, No 38 Gp Transport/Glider Towing sqn with A III and VII (1/46) at Great Dunmow (ex-Stirling IV). 1/46 renumbered No 295 Sqn. Codes G5-, L9- and 6S-

No 192 SQN

3/43, No 3 Gp ECM/Elint sqn, added B II (7/43) (to Wellington/Mosquito) at Gransden Lodge. 4/43 to Feltwell (No 2 Gp). 7/43 B V (3/44). 11/43 to Foulsham (No 100 Gp). 3/44 B III (BS) (8/45). 8/45 disbanded into CSE. Codes DT-

No 199 SQN

2/45, No 100 Gp ECM sqn, added B II (to Stirling) at North Creake. 7/45 disbanded. Codes EX-

No 202 SQN

10/46, postwar Coastal Command Met recce sqn formed through re-numbering of No 518 Sqn at Aldergrove. Codes Y3-

No 224 SQN

3/48, postwar Coastal Command Met recce sqn formed

at Aldergrove, took over No 202 Sqn det at Gibraltar. Last RAF Halifax sqn. Codes XB-

No 246 SQN

11/44, Transport Command sqn with C III (3/45). Added to Liberator (from No 511 Sqn nucleus). Replaced by Liberator, York, Skymaster. Codes unknown

No 295 SQN

2/43, No 38 Wing (Army Co-operation Command) glider tug sqn with Halifax A V (11/43) at Netheravon (ex-Whitley). 5/43 to Holmsley South, 6/43 to Hurn. Converted to Albemarles 10/43. Codes 8E- and 8Z-

No 295 SQN

1/46, postwar Transport Command glider tug sqn with Halifax A VII formed through re-numbering of No 190 Sqn. 4/46 re-numbered as No 297 Sqn. 9/47 re-formed at Fairford with A 9. 10/48 disbanded. Codes unknown

No 296 SQN

9/44, Allied Expeditionary Air Force (No 38 Gp) glider tug sqn with Halifax A V (2/45) at Brize Norton (ex-Albemarle). 9/44 to Earles Colne. 2/45 Halifax A III (1/46), 12/45 A VII (1/46). 1/46 disbanded. Codes 7C- and 9W-

No 297 SQN

10/44, Allied Expeditionary Air Force (No 38 Gp) glider tug sqn with Halifax A V (2/45) at Earls Colne (ex-Albemarle). 2/45 Halifax A III (4/46), 12/45 A VII (4/46). 4/46 disbanded. Codes L5- and P5-

No 297 SQN

4/46, postwar Transport Command glider tug sqn with Halifax A VII formed through re-numbering of No 295 Sqn. Re-equipped with HP Hastings 10/48. Codes MOHA-

No 298 SQN

11/43, No 38 Wing (Army Co-operation Command) glider tug sqn with Halifax A V (11/44) at Tarrant Rushton (ex-295 Sqn C Flt). 9/44 Halifax A III (7/45), 3/45 A VII (12/46). 7/45 to India. 12/46 disbanded. Codes 8A- and 8T-

No 301 ('POMERANIAN') SQN

11/44, Mediterranean Allied Air Forces special duties sqn with B II, B V (3/45) at Brindisi (ex-No 1586 Flt). 4/45 to Blackbushe to re-equip with Warwick. Codes unknown

No 301 ('POMERANIAN') SQN
1/46, postwar Transport Command sqn with C VIII (ex-Warwick). Codes GR-

No 304 ('SILESIAN') SQN
5/46, postwar Transport Command sqn with C VIII (ex-Warwick). Codes QD-

No 346 SQN (GB II/23 *GUYENNE*)
5/44, No 4 Gp Free French bomb sqn with B V (6/44) at Elvington. 6/44 B III (4/45), 3/45 B VI (11/45). 10/45 to Bordeaux-Merignac, 11/45 transferred to *Armée de l'Air*. Codes H7-

No 347 SQN (GB I/25 *TUNISIE*)
6/44, No 4 Gp Free French bomb sqn with B V (6/44) at Elvington. 7/44 B III (4/45), 3/45 B VI (11/45). 10/45 to Bordeaux-Merignac, 11/45 transferred to *Armée de l'Air*. Codes L8-

No 405 ('VANCOUVER') SQN, RCAF
4/42, No 4 Gp Canadian bomb sqn with B II (9/43) at Pocklington. 8/42 to Topcliffe, 10/42 to Beaulieu (Coastal Command), 1/43 transferred to No 6 (RCAF) Gp on formation, 3/43 to Topcliffe, 3/43 to Leeming, 4/43 to Gransden Lodge (No 8 Gp). 8/43 re-equipped with Lancaster. Codes LQ-

No 408 ('GOOSE') SQN, RCAF
9/42, No 5 Gp Canadian bomb sqn with B V (12/42) at Leeming (ex-Hampden). 12/42 B II (10/43). 1/43 No 6 (RCAF) Gp 8/43 to Linton-on-Ouse. 10/43-9/44 operated Lancaster II. 9/44 B III (2/45), 9/44 B VII (5/45). 5/45 cv'd to Lancaster. Codes EQ-

No 415 ('SWORDFISH') SQN, RCAF
7/44, No 6 (RCAF) Gp Canadian bomb sqn with B III (5/45) at East Moor. 3/45 B VII (5/45). 5/45 disbanded. Codes 6U-

No 419 ('MOOSE') SQN, RCAF
11/42, No 4 Gp Canadian bomb sqn with B II (4/44) at Croft. 11/42 to Middleton St George. 1/43 No 6 (RCAF) Gp. 3/44 to Lancaster. Codes VR-

No 420 ('SNOWY OWL') SQN, RCAF
12/43, No 6 (RCAF) Gp Canadian bomb sqn with B III (5/45) at Tholthorpe (ex-Wellington). 4/45 to Lancaster. Codes PT-

No 424 ('TIGER') SQN, RCAF
12/43, No 6 (RCAF) Gp Canadian bomb sqn with B III (1/45) at Skipton-on-Swale (ex-Wellington). 1/45 to Lancaster. Codes QB-

No 425 ('ALOUETTE') SQN, RCAF
12/43, No 6 (RCAF) Gp Canadian bomb sqn with B III (5/45) at Tholthorpe (ex-Wellington). 5/45 to Lancaster. Codes KW-

No 426 ('THUNDERBIRD') SQN, RCAF
4/44, No 6 (RCAF) Gp Canadian bomb sqn with B III (6/44) at Linton-on-Ouse (ex-Lancaster II). 6/44 B VI (5/45), 12/44 B III (5/45). 5/45 to Lancaster. Codes OW-

No 427 ('LION') SQN, RCAF
5/43, No 6 (RCAF) Gp Canadian bomb sqn with B V (2/44) at Leeming (ex-Wellington). 1/44 B III (3/45). 3/45 to Lancaster. Codes ZL-

No 428 ('GHOST') SQN, RCAF
6/43, No 6 (RCAF) Gp Canadian bomb sqn with B V (1/44) at Middleton St George (ex-Wellington). 11/43 B II (6/44). 6/44 to Lancaster. Codes NA-

No 429 ('BISON') SQN, RCAF
8/43, No 6 (RCAF) Gp Canadian bomb sqn with B II (1/44) at Leeming (ex-Wellington). 11/43 B V (3/44). 3/44 B III (3/45). 3/45 to Lancaster. Codes AL-

NO 431 (IROQUOIS) SQN, RCAF
7/43, No 6 (RCAF) Gp Canadian bomb sqn with B V (4/44) at Tholthorpe (ex-Wellington). 12/43 to Croft. 2/44 B III (10/44). 10/44 to Lancaster. Codes SE-

No 432 ('LEASIDE') SQN, RCAF
2/44, No 6 (RCAF) Gp Canadian bomb sqn with B III (7/44) at East Moor (ex-Lancaster II). 7/44 B VII (5/45). 5/45 disbanded. Codes QO-

No 433 ('PORCUPINE') SQN, RCAF
7/43, No 6 (RCAF) Gp Canadian bomb sqn with B III (1/45) at Skipton-on-Swale (newly-formed). 1/45 to Lancaster. Codes BM-

No 434 ('BLUENOSE') SQN, RCAF
6/43, No 6 (RCAF) Gp Canadian bomb sqn with B V (4/44) at Tholthorpe (newly-formed). 12/43 to Croft. 5/44 B III (12/44). 12/44 to Lancaster. Codes IP-

No 460 SQN, RAAF
8/42, No 1 Gp RAAF bomb sqn with B II (10/42) at Breighton (ex-Wellington). Conversion abandoned before sqn could become operational, and converted to Lancaster instead. Codes UV-

No 462 SQN, RAAF
9/42, Middle East Command RAAF bomb sqn with B II (2/44) at Fayid (from 10/227 and 76/462 dets). To LGs 237, 09, 167, 237, 167, Soluch, Gardabia, Hosc Raui, Terria and El Adem. 2/44 re-numbered as No 614 Sqn. Reformed 8/44 with B III (9/45) at Driffield as No 4 Gp RAAF sqn. 12/44 transferred to No 100 Gp as ABC jamming sqn, moved to Foulsham. 9/45 disbanded. Codes Z5-

No 466 SQN, RAAF
9/43, No 4 Gp RAAF bomb sqn with B II (11/43) at Leconfield (ex-Wellington). 11/43 B III (5/45). 6/44 to Driffield, 5/45 B VI (8/45). To Liberator. Codes HD-

No 502 ('ULSTER') SQN
2/43, No 19 Gp ASV sqn with GR II (3/45). 3/43 to St Eval (No 19 Gp), 6/43 to Holmsley South, 12/43 to St Davids, 9/44 to Stornoway (No 18 Gp). 3/45 GR III. Disbanded 25/5/45. Codes YG- and V9-

No 511 SQN
12/42, Lyneham Transport Command sqn, used B II for less than one month alongside Liberator and Albemarle. Codes unknown

No 517 SQN
11/43, Coastal Command No 19 Gp Met recce sqn with Met V (6/45) at St Davids (ex-Hudson, Hampden, Fortress). 2/44 to Brawdy, 3/45 Met III. 11/45 to Chivenor. 6/46 disbanded. Codes X9-

No 518 SQN
7/43, Coastal Command No 18 Gp Met recce sqn with Met V (6/45) at Stornoway. 9/43 to Tiree, 3/45 Met III. 9/45 to Aldergrove. 3/46 GR 6. 10/46 re-numbered as No 202 Sqn. Codes Y3-

No 519 SQN
8/45, postwar Coastal Command Met recce sqn with Met III. Disbanded 5/46. Codes Z9-

No 520 SQN
2/44, Coastal Command No 18 Gp Met recce sqn with Met V (5/45) at Gibraltar (with Hudson, Gladiator, Spitfire etc.). 5/45 Met III. 4/46 disbanded. Codes 2M-

No 521 SQN
12/45, postwar Coastal Command Met recce sqn with Met III. Disbanded 3/46. Codes 50-

No 578 SQN
1/44, No 4 Gp bomb sqn with B III (3/45) at Snaith (ex-C Flt No 51 Sqn). 2/44 to Burn. 4/45 disbanded. Codes LK-

No 614 ('COUNTY OF GLAMORGAN') SQN
Mediterranean Allied Air Forces bomb sqn with B II (3/45) at Celone (re-numbered from No 462 Sqn). 5/44 to Stornara, 7/44 to Amendola. Gradually replaced from 8/44 by Liberator. Codes unknown

No 620 SQN
5/45, postwar Transport Command glider tug sqn with A VII. To Aqir. Re-numbered as No 113 Sqn. Codes D4- and QS-, and postwar MOHC-

No 624 SQN
9/43, Mediterranean Air Command mixed Special Duties sqn, added B II (9/44) at Blida. 9/43 B V (2/44). 12/43 to Tocra. 9/44 disbanded. Codes unknown

No 640 SQN
1/44, No 4 Gp sqn with B III (3/45) at Leconfield (from C Flt No 158 Sqn). 3/45 B VI (5/45). 5/45 disbanded. Codes C8-

No 644 SQN
2/44, Allied Expeditionary Air Force (No 38 Group) glider tug sqn with A V (11/44) at Tarrant Rushton (from No 298 Sqn nucleus). 10/44 A III (6/45), 3/45 A VII (9/46). 12/45 Qastina. 8/46 A IX. 9/46 re-numbered as No 47 Sqn. Codes 2P- and 9U-, and postwar MOHD-

No 16 FERRY UNIT
Used Halifax and other types postwar from Dunkeswell, probably until 4/46. Codes unknown

No 21 HEAVY GLIDER CONVERSION UNIT
2/45, Horsa glider training unit formed at Brize Norton. Moved immediately to Elsham Wolds with Halifax tugs from 2/46. To North Luffenham 12/46. Disbanded 12/47. Codes FEP-, FEQ-, FER-, FES- and FET-

No 22 HEAVY GLIDER CONVERSION UNIT
Briefly used one Halifax at Blakeheath Farm before that type concentrated in No 21 HGCU. Codes unknown

No 28 HALIFAX CONVERSION FLIGHT
11/41, formed with B I at Leconfield. 1/42 combined with 107 CF to form No 1652 CU. Codes unknown

No 107 HALIFAX CONVERSION FLIGHT
12/41, authority to form with B I at Leconfield. No aircraft before 1/42, when combined with No 28 CF to form No 1652 CU. Codes unknown

No 241 OCU
1/48, re-designated from No 1665 HTCU. Received A IX on formation. Wfu early 1949. Codes unknown

No 301 SPECIAL DUTIES FLIGHT
7/43, formed with B V at Tempsford by re-designating Polish flight of No 138 Sqn. 11/43 to Tunis (No 344 Wing), then to Brindisi. 10/44 re-designated No 1586 Flt. Codes unknown

No 301 FERRY TRAINING UNIT
9/42, first Halifaxes received at Lyneham. 3/44 to Pershore. Absorbed by No 1 Ferry Unit. Codes unknown

No 1331 HEAVY TRANSPORT CONVERSION UNIT
12/46, formed from Halifax Training Unit at Dishforth. Absorbed by No 241 OCU 1/48. Codes unknown

No 1332 HEAVY TRANSPORT CONVERSION UNIT
11/45, absorbed Halifax A VII of No 1665 HTCU upon move to Dishforth. Became No 241 OCU. Codes YY- and OG-

No 1333 TRANSPORT SUPPORT TRAINING UNIT
10/45, equipped with A VII on move to Syerston. Became No 1333 HTSTU. 11/46 A IX. 7/47 to North Luffenham. Disbanded 1/48, aircraft transferred to No 241 OCU. Codes ODY-

No 1341 BOMBER SUPPORT FLIGHT
12/44, formed West Kirby, B III(BS). 2/45 to Digri, India. 5/45 amalgamated with No 159 Sqn (Liberators). 10/45 disbanded. Codes unknown

No 1361 METEOROLOGICAL FLIGHT
2/46. postwar Met unit. Aircraft and crews transferred to No 521 Sqn. Codes unknown

No 1361 TRANSPORT CONVERSION FLIGHT
2/46, possible intended re-designation of No 1361 (Met) Flt. Codes unknown

No 1383 TRANSPORT SUPPORT CONVERSION UNIT
8/45 Formed at Crosby with A VII. Disbanded 8/46. Codes GY-

No 1385 TRANSPORT SUPPORT CONVERSION UNIT
3/46, formed at Weathersfield with A III. 5/46 A VII. 7/46 disbanded. Aircraft transferred to No 1333 HTSTU. Codes unknown

No 1418 BOMBING DEVELOPMENT FLIGHT
1/42, formed from TR1335 *Gee* Development Unit at Boscombe Down. 4/42 to Feltwell, becoming No 1 Bombing Development Unit. 8/42 to Gransden Lodge. 8/42 to Newmarket. Disbanded 1947. Halifaxes used throughout unit's existence. Worked in association with Telecommunications Flying Unit at Hurn and (from 5/42) Defford. Also equipped with Halifax and Wellington. Codes (as No 1 BDU) OT-

No 1427 FLIGHT
no details

No 1445 FLIGHT
no details

No 1575 SPECIAL DUTIES FLIGHT
5/43, formed with B V at Tempsford (crews from No 161 Sqn). 6/43 to Maison Blanche, then Blida. 9/43 disbanded, transferring aircraft and crew to No 624 Sqn. Codes unknown

No 1577 TRIALS FLIGHT
8/43, formed with B V (and Lancaster) as part of No 221 Gp. Established in India by 10/43. 12/43 assigned to

transport duties. 3/44 to Chakeri, 5/44 to Mauripur. 11/44 B IIIs issued in place of Lancasters. 12/44 to Dhamal, 1/46 to Chakala. 5/46 disbanded. Codes unknown

No 1586 SPECIAL DUTIES FLIGHT
10/44, formed with B V at Brindisi from No 301 SD Flt. Became 301 Sqn 11/44. Codes unknown

No 1652 CONVERSION UNIT
1/42, No 4 Gp training unit with B II at Marston Moor, formed from Nos 28 and 107 Conversion Flts. 10/42 absorbed conversion flts of Nos 35 and 158 Sqns and became No 1652 HCU. 12/44 B III. 6/45 disbanded. Codes JA- and GV-

No 1654 HEAVY CONVERSION UNIT
9/43, No 5 Gp training unit replaced Manchesters with B II at Wigsley. Also reported as based at Swinderby. 1/44 replaced by Stirlings. Codes UG- and JR-

No 1656 HEAVY CONVERSION UNIT
10/42, No 4 Gp training unit with B II at Breighton Moor, formed from conversion flts of Nos 103 and 460 Sqns. 10/42 to Lindholme. Halifax gave way to Lancaster 11/42-11/43. Codes BL- and EK-

No 1658 HEAVY CONVERSION UNIT
10/42, No 4 Gp training unit with B I and II at Riccall, formed from conversion flts of Nos 10, 76, 78 and 102 Sqns. 9/44 B III. 4/45 disbanded, absorbed by No 1332 HTCU. Codes TT- and ZB-

No 1659 HEAVY CONVERSION UNIT
10/42, No 4 Gp training unit with B I and II at Leeming, formed from conversion flts of Nos 405 and 408 Sqns. 3/43 to Topcliffe. 9/44 B III. 9/45 disbanded. Codes FD-, FV- and RV-

No 1660 HEAVY CONVERSION UNIT
9/43, No 5 Gp training unit replaced Manchesters with B V at Swinderby. 1/44 replaced by Stirlings. Codes TV- and YW-

No 1661 HEAVY CONVERSION UNIT
9/43, No 5 Gp training unit replaced Manchesters with B II at Winthorp. Received some B III. 1/44 replaced by Stirlings. Codes GP- and KB-

No 1662 HEAVY CONVERSION UNIT
1/43, No 1 Gp training unit formed with Lancaster and B I, II and V at Blyton. Received some B III. 2/44 Lancaster flt moved to Hemswell as Lancaster Finishing School. Disbanded 4/45. Codes PE- and KF-

No 1663 HEAVY CONVERSION UNIT
3/43, No 4 Gp training unit with B II and V at Rufforth, formed with aircraft from other HCUs and new-build. 10/44 B III. 5/45 disbanded. Codes OO- and SV-

No 1664 (RCAF) HEAVY CONVERSION UNIT
5/43, No 6 Gp training unit with B II/V, formed at Croft. 12/43 to Dishforth. 11/44 re-named No 1664 (RCAF) HCU. 12/44 B III. 4/45 disbanded. Codes DH- and ZU-

No 1665 HEAVY CONVERSION UNIT
9/43, No 38 Gp training unit, added A V at Woolfox Lodge. 1/44 to Tilstock, 3/45 to Saltby, 8/45 to Marston Moor. Became No 1665 HTCU, with A III and C VI. 11/45 to Linton-on-Ouse. 7/46 disbanded and absorbed by No 1332 HTCU. Codes OG-

No 1666 HEAVY CONVERSION UNIT
6/43, No 6 Gp training unit with B II and V formed at Croft. 10/43 to Wombleton. Took over Lancaster task of co-located No 1679 HCU on disbandment of latter, 1/44. 4/44 Lancasters transferred to No 408 Sqn. 11/44 re-named No 1666 (RCAF) HCU. 11/44 B III, but re-equipped with Lancasters 1/44. Last Halifaxes left 3/45. Codes QY, and ND-

No 1667 HEAVY CONVERSION UNIT
8/43, No 5 Gp training unit formed with Lancaster and B II at Balderton. 11/43 replaced by Stirlings, and disbanded, becoming No 5 Lancaster Finishing School. Codes IG-

No 1669 HEAVY CONVERSION UNIT
9/44, No 5 Gp training unit formed with B II and B V at Langar. Received some B III, but Halifaxes replaced by Lancasters 12/44. Codes L6- and 6F-

No 1674 HEAVY CONVERSION UNIT
10/43, No 15 Gp (Coastal Command) training unit formed with Fortress, Liberator and Halifax II/V at Aldergrove. 10/43 to Longtown, 2/44 back to Aldergrove. 10/44 re-named No 1674 Training Wing. 8/45 to Milltown.

Received some Met III. Disbanded 11/45, passed aircraft to No 111 OTU. Codes OK-

No 111 OPERATIONAL TRAINING UNIT
Postwar training unit at Lossiemouth, took over Met training from No 1674 HCU 8/45. Disbanded 9/46. Codes H3-, X3- and 3G

No 1 (COASTAL) OPERATIONAL TRAINING UNIT
3/43, interim unit at Thornaby pending establishment of No 1674 HCU, using Halifax and Fortress. Codes unknown

AIRBORNE FORCES TACTICAL DEVELOPMENT UNIT
12/43, formed with Halifax, Whitley, Wellington at Tarrant Rushton. 1/44 to Netheravon. Became Air Transport Tactical Development Unit. Postwar, unit moved to Harwell, Brize Norton. Halifax withdrawn 1946. Codes unknown

ANTI-SUBMARINE WARFARE DEVELOPMENT UNIT
Occasional use of Halifax from Gosport during war and after. Last one wfu 3/47. Codes P9-

BOMB BALLISTICS DEVELOPMENT UNIT
Used Halifax during 1944, from Woodbridge. Codes unknown

BOMBER COMMAND INSTRUCTOR'S SCHOOL
12/44, B II (5/45) at Finningley, alongside Wellington and Lancaster. Codes IK- and IP-

BOMBING TRIALS UNIT
Some Halifaxes used from West Freugh during the war. Codes unknown

CENTRAL FLYING SCHOOL
Used at least one Halifax during 1944-45. Codes unknown

CENTRAL LANDING ESTABLISHMENT
10/41, B II glider tugs and paratroop transports at Haddenham (Thame). Later variants added during war. 3/46 to Upper Heyford. Became No 1 Parachute Training School. Moved to Henlow 1949. One A IX was the RAF's last Halifax in-service, written off 4/53. Codes unknown

CENTRAL GUNNERY SCHOOL
Used a B III at Catfoss postwar. Codes unknown

COASTAL COMMAND DEVELOPMENT UNIT
Occasional wartime trials/tactics development use of Halifax. Mainly from Thorney Island. Codes unknown

EMPIRE AIR NAVIGATION SCHOOL
No 1 Flight used 18 B IIIs from Shawbury postwar. Codes FGE-

EMPIRE RADIO SCHOOL
Used Halifax flying classrooms from Debden postwar. Codes FGF-

HALIFAX DEVELOPMENT FLIGHT
10/44, attached to No 246 Sqn at Holmsley South with B III. 3/45 Attached to No 187 Sqn. Assessed Halifax in transport role. Codes unknown

OPERATIONAL REFRESHER TRAINING UNIT
3/45, re-equipment with Halifaxes slowed down by Operation Varsity, but Stirling replaced by 5/45. Moved from Thruxton to Weathersfield 10/45, disbanded 1/46. Codes unknown

PATHFINDER FORCE NAVIGATION TRAINING UNIT
4/43, B II (9/44) at Gransden Lodge, alongside Stirling and Lancaster. Codes unknown

RADIO WARFARE ESTABLISHMENT
Postwar successor to No 192 Sqn, initially at Foulsham, then based at Watton from 10/45. Became Central Signals Establishment. Halifax wfu 1/47. Codes unknown

TRANSPORT COMMAND DEVELOPMENT UNIT
8/45, postwar unit using Halifax A III, C VIII, A VII, A IX from Brize Norton. To Abingdon 6/49, Halifax wfu. Codes unknown

APPENDIX B

HALIFAX IN RAF SERVICE
PARTIAL AIR ORDERS OF BATTLE

These air orders of battle include details of only those units flying Halifaxes – obviously Bomber Command included scores of units flying other types, as did the other Commands. They also exclude second-line units, except those flying Halifaxes

BOMBER COMMAND – MAY 1941

No 1 GROUP
Eight Wellington squadrons in Lincolnshire and Nottinghamshire

No 2 GROUP
Six Blenheim and one Wellington squadron at bases in Norfolk and Suffolk

No 3 GROUP
Ten Wellington, one Stirling and one mixed Stirling/Wellington squadron in Norfolk, Suffolk, Lincolnshire and Cambridgeshire

No 4 GROUP
Four Whitley, one Wellington squadron, plus;

No 35 Sqn	Halifax I	Linton-on-Ouse
No 76 Sqn	Halifax I	Leeming

No 5 GROUP
Three Manchester and five Hampden squadrons based in Lincolnshire

No 6 GROUP
Training group, Whitley and Wellington-equipped OTUs

No 7 GROUP
Training group with Blenheim and Hampden-equipped OTUs

BOMBER COMMAND – APRIL 1942

No 1 GROUP
Eight Wellington squadrons in Lincolnshire and Nottinghamshire, one partially equipped with Liberators

No 2 GROUP
Six Blenheim and two Boston squadrons at bases in Norfolk and Suffolk

No 3 GROUP
Nine Wellington, two Stirling and three mixed Stirling/Wellington squadrons in Norfolk, Suffolk, Lincolnshire and Cambridgeshire, plus;

No 138 Sqn	Halifax I, Whitley	Tempsford

No 4 GROUP
Four Whitley and one Wellington squadrons, plus;

No 10 Sqn	Halifax II, Whitley	Linton-on-Ouse
No 35 Sqn	Halifax II	Linton-on-Ouse
No 76 Sqn	Halifax II	Leeming
No 102 Sqn	Halifax II, Whitley	Topcliffe

No 5 GROUP
One Manchester, five Hampden, three Manchester/Lancaster, two Hampden/Manchester and one Hampden/Lancaster squadrons based in Lincolnshire

No 6 GROUP
Training group with Whitley and Wellington-equipped OTUs

No 7 GROUP
Training group with Blenheim, Hampden, Manchester and Wellington-equipped OTUs

BOMBER COMMAND – APRIL 1943

No 1 GROUP
Seven Wellington and one Lancaster squadrons in Lincolnshire and Nottinghamshire, plus;

No 103 Sqn	Halifax*	Elsham Wolds
No 460 Sqn	Halifax*, Wellington	Breighton
No 1662 HCU	Halifax/Manchester	Blyton

*both frontline units used Halifaxes for only a few months prior to re-equipping with the Lancaster

No 2 GROUP
Four Boston, three Ventura, three Mitchell and two Mosquito squadrons at bases in Norfolk and Suffolk

No 3 GROUP

One Wellington, one Lancaster, five Stirling, one mixed Wellington/Mosquito, one mixed Whitley/Lysander and one mixed Stirling/Wellington squadrons in Norfolk, Suffolk, Lincolnshire and Cambridgeshire, plus;

No 138 Sqn	Halifax I, Whitley	Tempsford

No 4 GROUP

One Whitley, four Wellington squadron, plus;

No 10 Sqn	Halifax II	Melbourne
No 51 Sqn	Halifax II, Whitley	Snaith
No 76 Sqn	Halifax II, V	Linton-on-Ouse
No 77 Sqn	Halifax II	Elvington
No 78 Sqn	Halifax II	East Moor
No 102 Sqn	Halifax II, Whitley	Topcliffe
No 158 Sqn	Halifax II	Driffield
No 1652 HCU	Halifax	Marston Moor
No 1658 HCU	Halifax	Riccall
No 1663 HCU	Halifax	Rufforth

No 5 GROUP

Eight Lancaster, one Wellington, and one Hampden/Manchester squadron based in Lincolnshire

No 6 (RCAF) GROUP

Six Wellington-equipped squadrons, plus;

No 405 Sqn	Halifax II	Leeming
No 408 Sqn	Halifax II	Skipton-on-Swale
No 419 Sqn	Halifax II	Middleton St George

No 8 (PFF) GROUP

One Lancaster, one Wellington and one Mosquito squadron, plus:

No 35 Sqn	Halifax II	Graveley

No 92 GROUP

Training group with Blenheim, Hampden, and Wellington-equipped OTUs

No 93 GROUP

Training group with Whitley and Wellington-equipped OTUs

COASTAL COMMAND

Coastal Command included Nos 15, 16, 17, 18 and 19 Groups, plus HQ RAF Iceland and HQ RAF Gibraltar. Only one Group included Halifaxes in its strength.

No 19 GROUP

Five Wellington, three Sunderland, two Beaufighter, one Catalina, one Liberator, and one Fortress squadron, plus;

No 58 Sqn	Halifax II, Whitley	Holmsley South
No 502 Sqn	Halifax II	Holmsley South

MEDITERRANEAN COMMAND

Mediterranean Command included AHQ North West Africa, AHQ Malta and AHQ Cyrenaica, Libya and Tunisia. The latter included two Halifax units, as detailed below;

No 178 Sqn	Halifax II, Liberator	Chemines
No 462 Sqn	Halifax II	Bir El Gardabia

BOMBER COMMAND – JULY 1944

No 1 GROUP

Nine Lancaster squadrons in Lincolnshire and Nottinghamshire;

No 1662 HCU	Lancaster, Halifax	Lindholme
No 1667 HCU	Halifax	Lindholme

No 3 GROUP

Two Stirling, six Lancaster, one mixed Wellington/Mosquito and one mixed Hudson/Lysander squadrons in Norfolk, Suffolk, Lincolnshire and Cambridgeshire, plus;

No 138 Sqn	Halifax II, V, Stirling	Tempsford
BBU	Halifax	Waterbeach

No 4 GROUP

No 10 Sqn	Halifax III	Melbourne
No 51 Sqn	Halifax III	Snaith
No 76 Sqn	Halifax III	Holme-on-Spalding Moor
No 77 Sqn	Halifax III	Full Sutton
No 78 Sqn	Halifax III	Breighton
No 102 Sqn	Halifax III	Pocklington
No 158 Sqn	Halifax III	Lissett
No 346 Sqn	Halifax III	Elvington
No 347 Sqn	Halifax III, V	Elvington
No 466 Sqn	Halifax III	Driffield
No 578 Sqn	Halifax III	Little Staughton
No 640 Sqn	Halifax III	Leconfield

No 1652 HCU	Halifax	Marston Moor
No 1658 HCU	Halifax	Marston Moor
No 1663 HCU	Halifax	Marston Moor

No 5 GROUP
Sixteen Lancaster squadrons based in Lincolnshire

No 6 (RCAF) GROUP
Three Lancaster-equipped squadrons, plus;

No 415 Sqn	Halifax III	East Moor
No 420 Sqn	Halifax III	Tholthorpe
No 425 Sqn	Halifax III	Tholthorpe
No 426 Sqn	Halifax III, VII	Linton-on-Ouse
No 427 Sqn	Halifax III	Leeming
No 429 Sqn	Halifax III	Leeming
No 431 Sqn	Halifax III	Croft
No 432 Sqn	Halifax III, VII	East Moor
No 433 Sqn	Halifax III	Skipton-on-Swale
No 434 Sqn	Halifax III	Croft
No 1659 HCU	Halifax	Topcliffe
No 1664 HCU	Halifax	Topcliffe
No 1666 HCU	Halifax	Topcliffe

No 8 (PFF) GROUP
Six Lancaster, and five Mosquito squadrons, plus;

| PFF NTU | Halifax, Lancaster | Warboys |

No 91 GROUP
Training group with Whitley and Wellington-equipped OTUs

No 92 GROUP
Training group with Wellington-equipped OTUs

No 93 GROUP
Training group with Wellington-equipped OTUs

No 100 GROUP
One Stirling, one Fortress, and two Mosquito squadrons in Norfolk, plus;

| No 192 Sqn | Halifax III/V, Wellington, Mosquito, Anson | Foulsham |

ALLIED EXPEDITIONARY AIR FORCE
Allied Expeditionary Air Force included Nos 38 and 85 Gps, and 2nd TAF (with Nos 2, 83 and 84 Gps and No 34 Wing). Only No 38 Gp included Halifaxes in its strength.

No 38 GROUP
Three Albemarle, and four Stirling squadrons, plus;

| No 298 Sqn | Halifax A V | Tarrant Rushton |
| No 644 Sqn | Halifax A V | Tarrant Rushton |

COASTAL COMMAND
Coastal Command included Nos 15, 16, 17, 18, 19, 106, and 247 Groups, plus HQ RAF Iceland and HQ RAF Gibraltar. Nos 15, 17, and 19 Groups and HQ Gibraltar included Halifaxes

No 15 GROUP (NORTHERN IRELAND)

| No 518 Sqn | Halifax Met V | Tiree |

No 17 GROUP (SCOTLAND)

| No 1674 Sqn det | Halifax | Croft |

No 19 GROUP (SOUTH WEST)

No 58 Sqn	Halifax GR II	St Davids
No 502 Sqn	Halifax GR II	St Davids
No 517 Sqn	Halifax Met V	St Eval

GIBRALTAR

| No 520 Sqn det | Halifax Met V, Hurricane | Gibraltar |

MEDITERRANEAN ALLIED AIR FORCES
Mediterranean Allied Air Forces included units in North Africa, Malta and Italy. It included two Halifax units, as detailed below;

No 148 Sqn	Halifax V	Brindisi
No 614 Sqn	Halifax II	Stornara
No 624 Sqn	Halifax II, Lysander	Blida
No 1586 Flight	Halifax, Liberator	Brindisi

AIR COMMAND SOUTH EAST ASIA

No 226 Group at Palam included a single Halifax unit, as detailed below;

| No 1577 Flight | Halifax | Cawnpore |

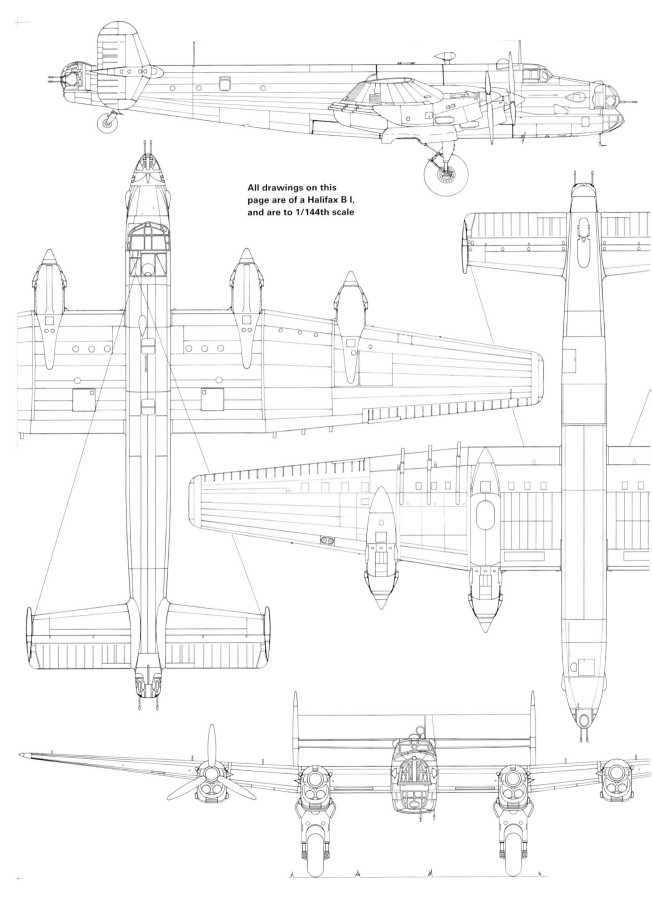

All drawings on this
page are of a Halifax B I,
and are to 1/144th scale

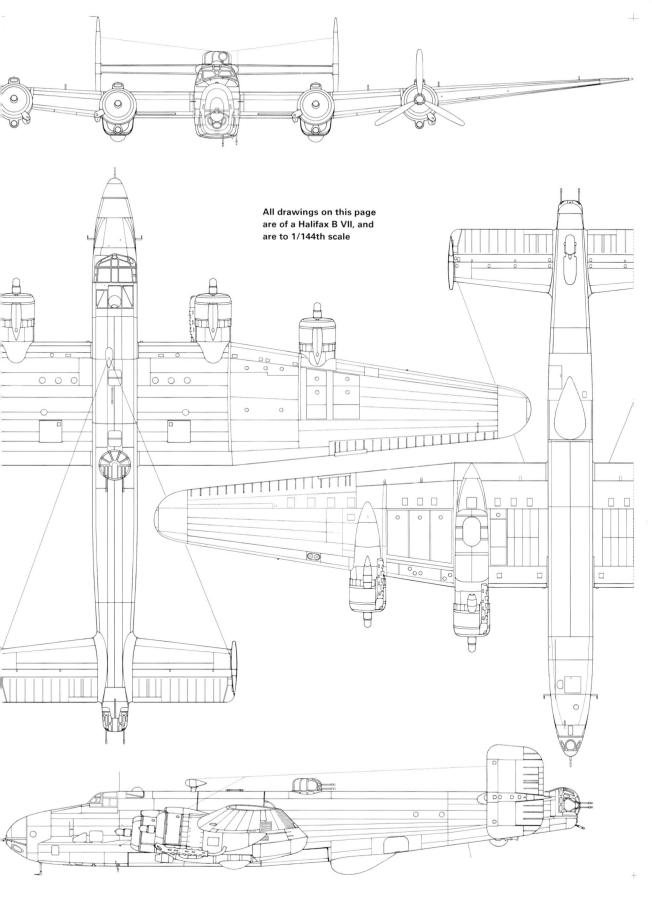

All drawings on this page
are of a Halifax B VII, and
are to 1/144th scale

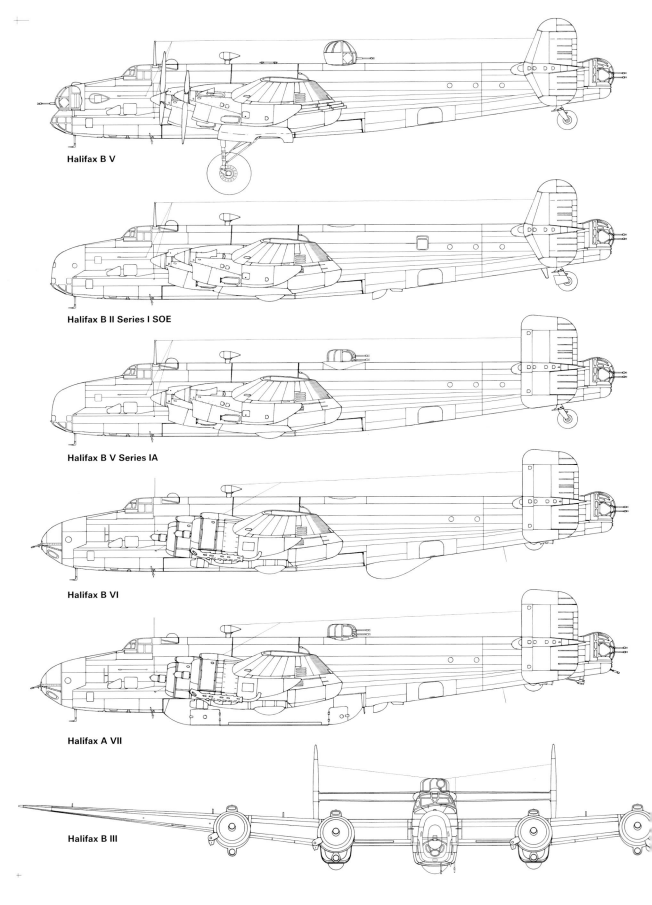

Halifax B V

Halifax B II Series I SOE

Halifax B V Series IA

Halifax B VI

Halifax A VII

Halifax B III

1

Halifax B II Series I (Special) BB324/ZA-X of No 10 Sqn, Melbourne, April 1943

Some of No 10 Sqn's first Halifax B Is were very early aircraft, retaining underwing fuel jettison pipes and beam gun hatches, rather than a mid-upper turret. These aircraft were soon replaced by more heavily-armed B IIs, which in turn gave way to the stripped and lightened B II Series I (Special). BB324 (formerly with No 76 Sqn) typified Halifax B IIs converted to Series I (Special) standards at unit level. As such, it should be compared with W1173 of No 405 Sqn, which was one of the factory-converted aircraft. This Halifax has had its mid-upper turret removed (as well as the nose turret), and has also lost its navigation blisters and gained the later close-fitting exhaust shrouds, but retains the early fixed landing light. The aircraft is fitted with Merlin XX engines with Gallay radiators, an enlarged oil cooler and associated 'lip' on the bottom of the intake. The small emblem below the cockpit is a terrier's head wearing a sailor's cap, above the legend 'Wings For Victory'. BB324 was lost during the raid on Mulheim on 23 June 1943.

2

Halifax B III HX323/ZA-C of No 10 Sqn, Melbourne, late 1944

HX233 still bore traces of its old No 35 Sqn identity (TL-M) and had completed 46 operations when taken over by Flg Off Charles Winter and his crew. Christened Charlie's Aunt, the aircraft's nose-art was applied by bomb-aimer Flt Sgt Arthur Smith, who copied a green-dressed Varga redhead from the magazine Esquire. The aircraft was damaged beyond repair (after it had been passed to No 1658 HCU at Riccall Common) on 10 December 1944, but the crew's luck held until landing after returning early from their 30th 'op' on 1 January 1945. Their new aircraft (LV785) clipped trees and crashed when its flaps retracted whilst trying to overshoot the runway following an engine failure – the accident claimed the lives of one of the gunners and the wireless operator. When some of No 4 Group's units adopted daylight tactical markings, No 10 seemed to have applied them using white chalk. Its temporary markings included a number of designs, including stripes and a hollow diamond.

3

Halifax B I Series I L9503/TL-P of No 35 Sqn, Linton-on-Ouse, Summer 1941

This No 35 Sqn Halifax was one of the first allocated to the unit, and was used on the historic raid on Kiel. Sometimes flown by Leonard Cheshire, the aircraft was deployed to Northolt on 21 July 1941 to be displayed for Winston Churchill and a delegation of Russian and Polish VIPs. Early Halifaxes exhibited a variety of detail differences in their camouflage schemes, before a standard, straight-edged, demarcation was adopted. This aircraft had a wavy demarcation between the upper surface disruptive camouflage and the black undersides. Aft of the wing trailing edge, the demarcation line ran diagonally up from the wingroot to the leading edge of the tailplane. This scheme should be compared with that applied to L9530 of No 76 Sqn, W7710 of No 405 Sqn and to No 35 Sqn sisters R9441 and W7676. L9503 was powered by original Merlin X engines, with the plain, forward-swept, intakes, and the original pattern exhaust pipes without fishtails. It was finally lost during a raid on Hamburg on 16 September 1941, having been in frontline service for almost a year.

4

Halifax B II Series I R9441/TL-S of No 35 Sqn, Linton-on-Ouse, Summer 1942

The first Halifax B IIs had a higher demarcation between the upper surface camouflage and the black undersides. Early aircraft had a hard, wavy, almost scalloped demarcation line, as seen on this aircraft (and on L9613 of No 138 Sqn). Optimised for production from sub-assemblies provided by diverse suppliers, the B II featured the Boulton Paul C Type mid upper turret. This particular aircraft was powered by Merlin XX engines with the lipped intakes and original pattern exhausts, but with the fishtail end. Very early aircraft retained twin aerial masts fore and aft above the fuselage, while later B IIs deleted the rearmost mast. No 35 Sqn contributed 18 Halifaxes to the 1000 Bomber Raid against Köln in May 1942. Following its tour with No 35 Sqn, R9441 saw further frontline action with No 102 Sqn, before passing to No 1652 HCU. It was written off with the latter unit on 4 April 1943 when it lost power on take-off from Marston Moor and the pilot feathered the wrong engine/propeller combination, causing the bomber to crash-land off the end of the runway.

5

Halifax B II Series I W7676/TL-P of No 35 Sqn, Graveley, Summer 1942

No 35 Sqn transferred from No 4 Group to help form the basis of the Path Finder Force (PFF) on 5 August 1942 – the PFF was formerly established as No 8 Group on 15 August 1942. No 35 Sqn (together with single Lancaster, Wellington, Stirling and Mosquito units) was subsequently joined by No 405 Sqn, and its Halifaxes, in 1943. This No 35 Sqn aircraft illustrates what was to become virtually the standard Halifax camouflage scheme for Bomber Command aircraft for most of the war. Later B II Series Is like W7676 had a straight, very hard-edged, demarcation line between the black undersides and the camouflaged upper surfaces. There was a slightly higher cutaway for the serial number, well aft. This aircraft should be compared with DG221 of No 10 Sqn. The last of No 35 Sqn's Halifaxes were even more modern looking, with the square-shaped fins associated with the B III and H2S. Such aircraft were typified by HR296/TL-L flown by Alec Cranswick. W7676 failed to return from an attack against Nuremburg on 28/29 August 1942.

6
Halifax B III LW497/MH-W of No 51 Sqn, Snaith, early March 1944
The sergeant in charge of Snaith's photo section was in great demand as an artist for producing nose-art, the topless girl ('Winsome WAAF') on the nose this Halifax III being a fine example of his work – this artwork was painted onto a sheet of canvas and stuck to the aircraft by way of adhesive tape, rather than being painted directly onto the bomber itself. That way it could be moved from aircraft to aircraft. Indeed, this nose art was worn by two other B IIIs: MZ794, lost on 29 January 1945 (by which time it had become MH-T), and MZ933. The latter aircraft was shot down over Belgium by a German nightfighter on 4 November 1944, the bomber taking with it the much-travelled 'Winsome WAAF' nose-art. Only two of the seven aircrew escaped the Halifax before it crashed. Returning to LW497 (which is unusual in having a Vickers VGO machine gun in the nose cone and no H2S radar bulge), this English Electric-built bomber was lost during a raid to Stuttgart on the night of 15/16 March 1944, the Halifax crashing south-east of the city. Again, only two of its seven-man crew succeeded in bailing out.

7
Halifax B III LV937/MH-E of No 51 Sqn, Snaith, 25 March 1945
By the end of March 1945, Bomber Command had 257 Halifax IIIs on charge, together with 151 Halifax VIs and 67 Halifax VIIs, in 16 squadrons, compared to 1373 Lancasters in 57 squadrons. Flt Lt R C Kemp and his crew flew 'Expensive Babe' on her 100th trip (the Osnabruck raid), making this B III (with H2S and mid-upper turret, but with no nose gun) one of the few Halifaxes to clock-up more than a 'century' of operational sorties. The aircraft had an exceptionally good finish, despite its age, although the bomb log was noticeably crooked. The swastika below the bomb log indicated a Ju 88 nightfighter shot down. The squadron flew its last bombing mission of the war (against Wangerooge) one month later, whilst LV937 was damaged beyond repair after suffering a collapsed tail wheel when it bounced on landing at High Ercall on 1 July 1945. The veteran bomber was Struck off Charge (SoC) three weeks later.

8
Halifax GR II Series IA JP328/BY-H of No 58 Sqn, St Davids, Summer 1944
This Halifax (which also served with No 502 Sqn as V9-H) retained its standard Bomber Command camouflage long after transfer to Coastal Command. Interestingly, though, this aircraft had grey codes and serials as per Coastal Command

practise, rather than the dull red codes and serials favoured by Bomber Command. The aircraft had its individual code letter repeated just aft of the nose glazing. JP328 was powered by Merlin 22 engines fitted with four-bladed airscrews on all four engines. The engines were housed in the later style nacelles, with the unlipped intakes and Morris Block radiators. The aircraft had extra bracing in the nose cone to support a single 0.50-in machine gun. Having survived almost a year in the frontline, JP328 was SoC on 6 May 1945 and sold for scrap.

9
Halifax GR II Series IA JP165/D of No 58 Sqn, Stornoway, early 1945
This Halifax GR II was one of those which wore full Coastal Command camouflage after transferring to Coastal Command. The aircraft had grey codes and serials, instead of the dull red codes and serials used by Bomber Command. It also wore only its individual code letter, and not the squadron's assigned BY- code prefix. The aircraft was fitted with four-bladed airscrews on all four engines, and had the extra bracing in the nose for a 0.50-in machine gun. This aircraft was lost on 9 April 1945 when it flew into high ground whilst in cloud near Tarbert, in the south of the Western Isles.

10
Halifax B I Series I L9530/MP-L of No 76 Sqn, Middleton St George, August 1941
Delivered to No 35 Sqn on 3 June 1941, this Halifax B I Series I was transferred to No 76 three days later, and flew its first operation on 19 July 1941. The aircraft was in the earliest configuration, with Merlin X engines in the original nacelles, and the original plain and earliest pattern exhausts. The Captain for this sortie was Plt Off Ireton, but Christopher Cheshire took over for subsequent missions on 30 July (against Köln) and 2 August (Berlin). L9530 is shown as it appeared returning from its fourth mission. It was shot down on its fifth, on the night of 12/13 August. The Captain, again Flt Lt Christopher Cheshire, was the brother of Leonard Cheshire, who later commanded No 76 Sqn. Christopher Cheshire survived the war as a PoW, along with four of the six remaining crew. The mid-upper and tail gunners were killed. The aircraft carried a mock heraldic crest which included a block of cheese, a cat and other elements which referred to Cheshire's name. Early Halifaxes were delivered with this high wavy demarcation line between the upper surface disruptive camouflage and the black lower surfaces.

11
Halifax B III LW648/MP-A of No 76 Sqn, Holme-on-Spalding Moor, Autumn 1944
In all Halifax squadrons, whether RCAF, RAAF or RAF, aircrew tended to be of diverse nationalities, usually mixed even within individual crews. But even in the multi-national wartime Bomber Command, with its legions of Colonial and

Dominion aircrew, Nigerians were a rarity. No-one had heard of political correctness, so with a Nigerian wireless operator, the crew of LW648 naturally named 'their' Halifax *'Achtung! The Black Prince'*. The bomb log used red paint for night operations, and yellow for daylight raids, which were clearly becoming more common by this stage of the war. The aircraft failed to return from a raid on Bochum on 4 November 1944.

12

Halifax B V Series IA LL126/KN-W of No 77 Sqn, Elvington, Winter 1943

Merlin XX-engined Halifax B IIs and B Vs had inadequate performance, even in lightened, reduced drag, Series IA and Series I Special form. This aircraft has the later rectangular tailfins usually associated with the Hercules-engined variants of the Halifax, plus a single 0.303-in machine gun in the nose glazing for use by the bomb-aimer. It also features Morris Block radiators and the final style of exhaust shrouds, but neither H2S nor a ventral gun turret. 'W-William' of No 77 Sqn has an appropriate name and nose-art, *"Oor Wullie"*, which almost certainly reflects the Scottish origins of its pilot. Following service with this unit, LL126 spent time with French-manned Nos 346 and 347 Sqns at Elvington soon after their formation in the spring of 1944, before being passed to second-line unit No 1662 HCU at Blyton. The bomber was subsequently lost when it dived into the ground at Long Ashton, near Bristol, during a night navigation exercise on 21 November 1944.

13

Halifax B II Series I DG221/EY-A of No 78 Sqn, Middleton St George, July 1942

This No 78 Sqn Halifax, with Merlin XX engines, associated 'lipped' intakes and fishtail exhausts, was sent to Boscombe Down after completing only ten operations for trials aimed at investigating the reasons for the declining performance of some in-service Halifaxes. One of the key reasons in DG221's case was a particularly rough coat of RDM2A Night paint on the undersurfaces. Interestingly, the demarcation line between the upper and lower surface colours was noticeably 'soft', as though never properly masked. After the tests, the aircraft returned to No 78 Sqn, and later passed to No 1658 HCU, but it had served its purpose, and laid the groundwork for the Series I (Special) and Series IA. Much later in the war, No 78 Sqn applied daylight tactical markings on the fins of its Halifax IIIs, these consisting of pairs of thin white horizontal lines top and bottom. DG221 was written off at Riccall on 30 November 1943 when it suffered an undercarriage failure upon landing.

14

Halifax B II Series I L9613/NF-V of No 138 (Special Duties) Sqn, detached to Fayid, Egypt, December 1942

L9613 was an early B II Series I converted for SOE and Polish Home Army support operations, with a paratroop door in the floor immediately aft of the bomb bay, a deflector to prevent containers from striking the tailwheel, a sheet-metal wheel guard to stop static lines from snagging the tailwheel and no mid-upper gun turret. The aircraft had Merlin X engines and early Gallay radiators in the original plain intakes, and retained standard bomber camouflage -- albeit with a very high 'scalloped' demarcation line. Three aircraft (including L9612 and L9613) were hastily converted at Ringway in October 1941 to give the SOE an aircraft capable of dropping supplies and agents as far afield as Poland. 'Bomber' Harris begrudged diverting the aircraft from the bomber force, although No 138 Squadron's strength was raised to five Halifaxes in January 1942. On the night of 28/29 December 1941 this aircraft, captained by Sqn Ldr (then Flt Lt) Ron Hockey, dropped the SOE team which assassinated Reinhardt Heydrich. Hockey subsequently took command of No 138 Sqn. L9613 survived its many varied sorties over Occupied Europe to be passed to second line unit No 1661 HCU at Winthorpe, who in turn eventually handed it over to Blyton-based No 1662 HCU. It was written off with the latter unit when it belly-landed at Blyton on 20 April 1944.

15

Halifax B V Series I (Special) DG253/NF-F, of No 138 (Special Duties) Sqn, Tempsford, September 1943

Missions to Poland represented the extreme limit of the Halifax's range, even with long-range tanks, and every effort was made to reduce the weight and drag of SOE aircraft. The normal nose turret of B II or B V Series Is was replaced by a simple streamlined metal fairing, known as the Tempsford or Z-type nose. The modified aircraft also lost their underwing fuel jettison pipes, fin de-icer boots, balloon cable-cutters, flare chute fairings, navigation blisters and various ice guards, hand rails and antennas. The engine exhaust shrouds were removed, and the exhausts were instead painted with heat-absorbing paint. This modification package was subsequently adopted by some Bomber Command Halifaxes, although these often retained mid-upper gun turrets. This aircraft wore standard bomber camouflage, but unlike L9613, had a windbreak fairing (known as an exit cone) around the new paratroop hatch. It also had the tailwheel shrouded in sheet aluminium. On SOE (and other long-range) aircraft, outboard engines were often fitted with four-bladed propellers, but not DG253. The B V's weight restrictions made the type a natural choice for SOE, Coastal Command and transport operations. This aircraft was shot down into the sea by flak near Harlingen on 29 September 1943, the rear gunner continuing to exchange fire with the AAA battery until impact.

16

Halifax B II Series IA JP246/FS-B of No 148

(Special Duties) Sqn, Derna, September 1943

An ex-No 624 Sqn aircraft, this Special Operations-equipped B II Series IA had the rectangular tailfins and glazed nose normally associated with the later Hercules-powered Halifax variants, as well as Merlin XX engines in the later nacelles and Morris Block radiators. With no armament apart from the tail turret, and with a tailwheel guard and an exit cone, this Halifax was typical of late-war SOE aircraft, and surprisingly lacked the normal (for No 148 Sqn) Desert Air Force colour scheme, with mid-stone replacing dark green on the topsides. A veteran of many Special Duties operations, JP246 was written off when it swung on landing and had its undercarriage collapse at Brindisi after completing a clandestine sortie on 8 October 1944

17

Halifax B III LV917/NP-C of No 158 Sqn, Lissett, April 1945

Two of No 158 Sqn's aircraft were actually delivered to the unit on Friday, 13 March 1944 (although RAF records show official dates of 10 and 7 March). These were LV907 and LV917, which had amassed 128 and 99 operational missions, respectively, by VE-Day. Both aircraft also flew on No 158 Sqn's last mission of the war, when the unit attacked coastal batteries at Wangerooge on 25 April 1945. LV907 duly 'became famous', and was exhibited in Oxford St in June 1945, wearing the name 'FRIDAY THE 13th' and a host of other usually unlucky symbols. LV917 'Clueless' retired with rather less of a fanfare. The aircraft had nose-art featuring a Gremlin, and had a row of medal ribbons won by the crew, in addition to its '100-up' bomb log. Like LV917, 'Clueless' had two diagonal yellow stripes on its outer fin faces, although No 158 Sqn also used yellow fins and black rudders as its daylight tactical marking. having served together for over a year in the frontline, both aircraft were SoC on 18 May 1945.

18

Halifax B III (BS) MZ971/6Y-E of No 171 Sqn, North Creake, early 1945

Formed in September 1944, No 171 Sqn was a dedicated Radar Countermeasures unit, initially operating a mix of specially-equipped Halifaxes and Stirlings. The squadron's aircraft (like those of the co-located No 199 Sqn) were equipped with Mandrel, a sophisticated airborne jamming system which proved highly effective against German early warning radar. It allowed aircraft to penetrate under the so-called 'Mandrel screen', using window to confuse shorter-range German radars. Mandrel-equipped aircraft like MZ971 were distinguishable by an array of antennae along the belly of the aircraft. Unlike No 192 Sqn, No 171 had no Elint role. Usually flown by Wt Off Jamieson, RAAF, and his crew, MZ971 was decorated with a typical pin-up and the legend 'I'm Easy!'. It also carried an impressive log of missions completed. MZ971 moved to No 11 Ferry Unit postwar, and was SoC on 26 October 1945.

19

Halifax B III (BS) serial unknown/DT-G of No 192 Sqn, Foulsham, late 1944

No 100 Group always preferred the Halifax to the Lancaster because it provided its specialist operators with a more capacious and comfortable working environment, while also providing better access to 'black boxes'. By the end of the war, great efforts were being made to standardise Main Force bomber squadrons on the Lancaster, providing a surplus of Halifaxes for use by Bomber Support, Coastal Command and Airborne Forces units. The Halifax had been designed from the outset as a 'General Purpose' bomber, and it proved a better aircraft than the Lancaster in all but the straight night-bombing role. 'Sleepy Gal' was a typical late-war Halifax, with only a discrete array of whip antennas revealing her Elint role. Despite No 192 Sqn's secretive task, the unit's aircraft often wore colourful nose-art and individual aircraft names. Conversely, the unit's early Halifaxes had been extremely anonymous, often operating without even unit codes, and certainly without such fripperies as nose-art. One of the squadron's Australian pilots (Flt Lt Matthews) flew one of the most strikingly decorated Halifaxes in Bomber Command, with an enormous Kangaroo insignia and more than 50 miniature Kangaroos as mission markings.

20

Halifax B III (BS) PN431/DT-A of No 192 Sqn, Foulsham, March 1945

'Angel', another No 192 Sqn Halifax decorated with a scantily-clad maiden, was regularly flown by the CO, Wg Cdr Donaldson, at the start of 1945. The unit flew independent Elint operations (using single aircraft or larger formations), 'spoof' raids dropping Window in order to draw up fighters, and RCM and Elint missions in support of Main Force bomber operations. The independent 'spoof' raids (known as 'Foulsham Follies') could sometimes draw up as many as 150 nightfighters – about ten of which could usually be relied upon to crash on landing, thus making No 192's Halifaxes more effective than many dedicated Intruder aircraft! The squadron frequently carried up to six 500-lb bombs in the wing bays of its aircraft, in addition to their more specialised role equipment. This aircraft was SoC on 18 October 1945.

21

Halifax A V DG396/QQ, of No 295 Sqn during Operation Elaborate (UK-North Africa glider ferry), No 38 Wing, Army Co-operation Command, Holmsley South, June 1943

Although its role necessitated flights from the UK, via Gibraltar, to Salé, in Morocco, No 295 Sqn normally retained standard European Bomber Command camouflage on its Halifaxes, rather than the North African theatre bomber camouflage in which mid-stone replaced the areas of dark green – DG396 was an exception, boasting the less common desert scheme. On 17 September 1943, this aircraft, towing a Horsa glider, was attacked by eight Ju 88s. Its pilot, Flg Off Norman, refused to jettison his glider, and skilfully evaded cannon and rocket fire from the Ju 88s. The glider crew released themselves to give Norman a better chance, and he made it to Salé on three engines following two rocket hits. His tail-gunner, Sgt Grant, received a DFM for shooting down one of the attackers, while Norman received a DFC. The aircraft had Merlin XX engines inboard, driving three-bladed propellers, with Merlin 22s and four-bladed propellers outboard. Interestingly, all the engines were housed in the mid-period nacelles, with Gallay radiators and the distinctive 'lipped' intakes. Following the completion of its service with No 295 Sqn, DG396 was passed to No 148 (Special Duties) Sqn and eventually SoC on 1 April 1945.

22
Halifax B III LL573/L8-B of No 347 Sqn, Elvington, Early 1945

The RAF formed a Free French bomber wing at RAF Elvington in May/June 1944, consisting of Nos 346 and 347 Sqns. The former unit was established first on 16 May (utilising personnel from French North Africa) whilst No 347 Sqn followed on 20 June - both units briefly operated Merlin-engined Mk V Halifaxes. This later B III carries No 347 Sqn's red diamond fin insignia and L8 codes (Nos 102, 346, 347 and 640 are known to have also adopted yellow-outlined codes). Some squadron aircraft latterly carried the unit's bison badge on the nose, but LL573 has only the Free French Cross of Lorraine on the nose. The RAF's French-crewed Halifaxes wore French roundels and fin flashes in the same locations as RAF insignia would normally have been applied. No 347 Sqn took over the traditions *of Groupe de Bombardement 1/25 'Tunisie'*, whilst No 346 Sqn took over the traditions of *Groupe de Bombardement 2/23 'Guyenne'*, including adorning its Halifaxes with the unit's white rabbit insignia on a blue and orange disc, outlined in red. By this stage of the war, the use of H2S was virtually universal on Bomber Command Halifaxes, although No 347 Sqn ended the conflict still using a number of B IIIs with the Preston-Green ventral gun turret, including this aircraft. Some 64 Halifaxes were transferred to the *Armée de l'Air* between the end of the war and 21 August 1947. LL573 was not one of those aircraft supplied to the French postwar, however, as it suffered an engine fire in flight on 17 February 1945 and was not repaired upon carrying out an emergency landing. It was duly SoC on 25 July 1945.

23
Halifax B II Series I W7710/LQ-R of No 405 Sqn, RCAF, Topcliffe, Summer 1942

'RUHR VALLEY EXPRESS' was amongst the original batch of aircraft allocated to No 405 Sqn, and it was used on the unit's first mission. As the first RCAF Halifax squadron, No 405 transferred from No 4 Group to the Canadian No 6 Group on 1 January 1943. The squadron subsequently moved to No 8 Group, after which it converted to the Lancaster. This aircraft has an unusually high, but straight and hard-edged, demarcation between upper and lower surface colours, similar in position to the early 'scalloped' demarcation line. It was powered by Merlin XX engines and had the lipped intakes associated with the enlarged oil cooler. This aircraft failed to return from an attack on Flensburg on 2 October 1942.

24
Halifax B II Series I (Special) W1173/LQ-X of No 405 Sqn, RCAF, Topcliffe, Summer 1942

'Xcalibur' was one of the first aircraft converted by Handley Page at Rawcliffe to Series I (Special) standard, with a Z-type nose fairing replacing the normal front turret – it initially retained its Hudson-type mid-upper turret. The aircraft wore a small gold sword badge, the name *'Xcalibur'* and a small red maple leaf device below the cockpit. The Halifax bomber is closely associated with the Canadian-manned No 4 Group in Yorkshire, and some 15 frontline RCAF squadrons in Britain operated the type at one time or another. This compared with only 13 RAF home-based bomber squadrons and three further RAF squadrons with No 100 Group, as well as two Free French and three RAAF units.

25
Halifax B III LW119/QB-O of No 424 Sqn, RCAF, Topcliffe, November 1944

'Oscar' was one of the most colourfully-marked Lancasters in Bomber Command, with a huge representation of its eponymous hero and a gaudy bomb log. The Halifax formed the backbone of the Canadian No 6 Group for most of the war, although nine of the squadrons (including No 424) had re-equipped with Lancasters by the end of the war – only Nos 408, 415, 425, 426 and 432 remained wholly Halifax-equipped. This aircraft was broadly representative of most frontline Halifaxes at the tail end of 1944, with ventral H2S, a dorsal gun turret and a VGO machine gun in the nose, although it lacked a DF loop. LW119 was passed to No 187 (Transport) Sqn in January 1945 when No 424 Sqn commenced its conversion onto the Lancaster. It was finally SoC on 7 October 1946.

26
Halifax B III MZ620/KW-T of No 425 Sqn, RCAF, Tholthorpe, November 1944

In November 1944, when official RCAF photographers visited Tholthorpe, in North Yorkshire, No 425 Sqn included roughly equal numbers of Halifax IIIs with ventral H2S radar and Preston Green gun turrets. All of the aircraft had dorsal gun turrets, but none had the optional VGO machine gun in the nose. This particular aircraft was later passed to No 1664 HCU and then placed in storage when the latter unit disbanded in April 1945. It was finally SoC on 24 September 1946.

No 425 'Alouette' Sqn was a French Canadian unit, and remains extant to this day, now flying CF-188 Hornets.

27
Halifax B VII NP808/-E of No 426 Sqn, RCAF, (ex-No 424 Sqn) Linton-on-Ouse, early 1945

The Halifax B VII was an interim version, being effectively a B VI with the original Hercules engines of the basic B III. It was used principally, but not exclusively, by Nos 408, 415, 426 and 432 Sqns. This aircraft is seen as it appeared after being transferred from No 424 Sqn, with that unit's QB- codes painted out, and with the new OW- codes of No 426 Sqn applied in chalk. NP808 ended its days with the Signals School in July 1948. The Halifax B VI was broadly equivalent to the late B III, with H2S permanently installed and with extended wingtips. It also had grouped pressure transfer fuel tanks, extra fuel tankage and new carburettor air intake filters. The aircraft also boasted new 1675 shp Hercules 100 engines, which dramatically improved performance. It was designed with hot-and-high operations in the Far East in mind, and relatively few B VIs reached the frontline before the war ended.

28
Halifax B V Series IA LK640/SE-Q of No 431 Sqn, RCAF, Tholthorpe, Summer 1943

Despite the Rootes and Fairey-built B V's new Dowty undercarriage imposing a 40,000-lb maximum landing weight limit, the type was extensively used as a bomber, although many B Vs were soon converted for other roles too. Primarily associated with the Hercules-engined Halifax variants, many RCAF squadrons initially flew Merlin-engined B IIs and B Vs. This aircraft (lost attacking Ludwigshafen on 19 November 1943) had a small picture of 'Queenie' (the phonetic aircraft code letter) on the nose and carried the crew's nicknames in oblique capitals next to their respective stations, including 'DAVE' (Bomb Aimer), 'LORNE' (W/Op), 'BOB' (navigator), 'BILL' (pilot) and 'MAC' (Flight engineer). Although a Series IA, with Merlin XX engines, Morris Block radiators and the later glazed nose fairing, LK640 retained the original 'triangular' tailfins, and lacked H2S or a Preston Green ventral turret.

29
Halifax B II Series I W1169/S of No 462 Sqn, RAAF, No 249 Wing, Hosc Raui, September 1943

No 462 Sqn was formed under the command of Wg Cdr D O Young DSO, DFC, AFC on 6 September 1942 through the amalgamation of detachments of Nos 10 and 76 Sqns. The unit initially flew B II Series Is in standard Bomber Command camouflage, although the dark green on the top-surfaces was soon replaced by mid-stone. Later, the old B II Series Is were replaced by Series I (Specials) and eventually by Series IAs, some equipped with H2S. Originally fitted with a mid-upper turret and standard nose turret, W1169

eventually had the mid-upper turret removed, and the nose turret de-activated and stripped of armament, then sealed with doped canvas to save weight and reduce drag. Removal of the front guns was relatively common on No 462 Sqn aircraft, but the canvas shrouding was distinctly non-standard. This aircraft completed over 50 missions with the Australian unit.

30
Halifax B III (BS) MZ913/Z5-N of No 462 Sqn, RAAF, Foulsham, April 1945

Formerly with No 434 Sqn, 'Jane' was flown by Flt Lt Ron Hines of No 462 Sqn during the Spring of 1945, this unit being the third of No 100 Group's Halifax squadrons – it was used primarily on *Airborne Cigar* (ABC) operations, jamming German nightfighter control frequencies and carrying a Special Operator, usually German-speaking, and often German-born. The ABC-equipped Halifaxes had two huge transmitter antenna masts above the fuselage, and another below, in addition to a number of whip receiver antennae. By the end of the war, 11 of No 462's Halifaxes were equipped with ABC. The squadron retained the vertical yellow fin stripes it had used as daylight tactical markings despite switching from No 4 to No 100 Group. MZ913 survived the war and was SoC on 14 March 1947.

31
Halifax B III HX266/HD-E of No 466 Sqn, RAAF, Driffield, late 1944

Like so many Australian Bomber Command units, No 466 Sqn decorated many of its Halifaxes with nose-art. Perhaps the most photographed were LW172/HD-F 'Get Up Them Stairs', with *Popeye* and *Olive Oil* on the nose, RG596/HD-T 'Trixie', or Flt Lt S P Kelly's NA169/HD-A 'Kelly's Gang Ride Again (+8¼)', although there were many others. This aircraft, with the quaint motto 'There oughta be more time for love' had bomb logs in the form of inverted pyramids, as well as two swastikas representing nightfighter kill claims. Sister *aircraft 'Facta non Verba'* used pyramid-shaped bomb logs too. When daylight tactical markings were introduced, No 466 Sqn used horizontal bands across the tailfins, as shown. Following its long tour with the Australian unit, HX266 was passed to No 1658 HCU before finally being SoC on 8 February 1947.

32
Halifax GR II Series I (Special) HR686/J2 of No 502 Sqn, St Eval, Summer 1944

Cunliffe-Owen converted a number of B II Series I (Specials) for service with Coastal Command, often with ASV 3 radar in a ventral radome similar to that used by H2S on bomber aircraft. Many aircraft also had four-bladed propellers for improved long-range performance, sometimes only on the outboard engines, like HR686. This aircraft carries a 0.50-in 'scare gun' in the nose cone, and has the early AV III turret installation, with a bulky raised fairing to allow greater depression. Many early Coastal Command Halifaxes were delivered to their new squadrons still wearing standard Bomber Command camouflage, unlike HR686, which wears standard Coastal Command colours. This aircraft failed to return from a patrol on 3 October 1944.

33
Halifax Met V Series IA LL469/X9-W of No 517 Sqn, Brawdy, Spring 1945

Unusually for a meteorological Halifax, this No 517 Sqn aircraft was fitted with a ventral Preston-Green gun turret, which it retained even after retirement to No 1674 HCU, the final operator of large numbers of ex-Coastal Command Halifaxes. The aircraft had Merlin 22 engines in the late-pattern nacelles, driving four-bladed propellers all-round. It wore standard Coastal Command camouflage, albeit with a slightly lower demarcation than usual, and had no mid-upper turret fitted. LL469 was SoC on 8 June 1945.

34
Halifax Met III LV876/X9-F of No 517 Sqn, Brawdy, Spring 1945

The easy availability of surplus Merlin-engined Halifaxes – especially the weight-limited Mk Vs – led to their widespread use in 'second-line' roles. In fact, the Merlin was not well-suited to typical Meteorological flight profiles either, which involved a long, low-boost cruise followed by a rapid climb, and engine failures were common. Eventually, the meteorological squadrons began to receive surplus Bomber Command Mk IIIs (and even Mk VIs) converted for the role. These tended to lack ventral radar or gun turrets, with the exception of the tail turret. The re-equipment process did not begin until early 1945, and only small numbers of Met IIIs entered service with Nos 502, 517 and 518 Sqns before VE-Day. LV876 retained full Bomber Command camouflage (having survived operations with Nos 76, 78 and 51 Sqns), albeit with Coastal Command grey codes and serials, including a small repetition of the individual code letter high on the nose. Halifax Met VIs (re-designated as GR 6s) were the last examples of the breed in RAF service, with No 224 Sqn relinquishing its last aircraft in early 1952. War-weary LV876 had long since been disposed of by then, however, being SoC on 20 August 1946.

35
Halifax Met V Series IA LK966/P of No 518 Sqn, Stornoway, early 1944

Although painted in standard Coastal Command camouflage, LK966 was non-standard in many ways. The demarcation between the white undersides and plain dark sea grey (not temperate camouflage) topsides was much higher than usual, leaving the entire engine nacelles in white, and giving only a tiny thin grey stripe along the fuselage 'roof'. The aircraft also had black codes and serials, rather than the more usual grey – No 518 Sqn did not apply its assigned Y3-code

letters until the end of the war. A fairly early meteorological conversion, LK966 had neither ventral radar nor gun turret, and had no window behind the nose-mounted psychrometer either. It had three-bladed propellers on all four engines, although the latter boasted later pattern air intakes associated with the Morris Block radiator. Following its spell with No 518 Sqn, LK966 was transferred to No 520 Sqn on Gibraltar. The aircraft was subsequently lost on 24 November 1944 when its crew had to ditch north-west of the Cape St Vincent, on the Portuguese coast, following engine failure during a met flight.

36
Halifax Met V Series IA LK960/2-L of No 520 Sqn, Gibraltar, Summer 1944

A late Met V, LK960 had Merlin 22 engines with Morris Block radiators and four-bladed propellers all-round, and a small rectangular window behind the nose-mounted psychrometer. Most Meteorological Halifaxes did not carry a nose-mounted gun, and even when a gun was fitted it tended to be a 0.303-in Browning, and not a heavier 0.50 cal machine gun as used in the anti-submarine Coastal Command Halifaxes. Like LK966, this aircraft was transferred to No 520 Sqn, although it survived the war to be SoC shortly after VE-Day, on 14 May 1945.

37
Halifax B III LK797/LK-E of No 578 Sqn, Burn, 30 March 1944

Only one Halifax aircrew member won the RAF's supreme award of the Victoria Cross for a single act of gallantry. Cyril (better known as 'Cy' or 'Joe') Barton met his end in this aircraft after crashing near Ryhope Colliery, south of Sunderland, after returning from a raid on Nuremberg. Attacked by a Ju 88 and an Me 410, the aircraft was badly damaged, and the bomb-aimer, navigator and wireless operator bailed out, but Barton struggled back to save the remaining members of his crew, who survived the crash. Nose-art had been designed for Barton's aircraft, but at the time of the crash had been applied only in chalk, as shown. A schoolboy who witnessed the aftermath of the crash subsequently befriended the crew, and this illustration is based on his and their memories. Another Halifax pilot, Leonard Cheshire, received a VC in recognition of his extraordinary career, which included two Halifax tours and single tours on the Whitley and Lancaster.

38
Halifax A V Series IA (serial unknown)/9U-K of No 644 Sqn, No 38 Group, Tarrant Rushton, D-Day, 6 June 1944

No 644 Sqn was formed from a nucleus provided by No 298 Sqn's C Flight in March 1944. In preparation for the invasion of Europe, both squadrons added Gee and Rebecca Mk II navaids to their aircraft, and replaced Merlin XX engines with more serviceable Merlin 22s. At much the same time, three-bladed propellers were replaced by four-bladed units, although aircraft with three-blade airscrews were still common on D-Day itself, including the subject of this profile. As 6 June dawned, No 644 Sqn was still in the process of re-coding its aircraft. Some wore the original single-letter aircraft codes, others the three-digit codes with the squadron prefix 2P-, and yet others the new prefix 9U-. Merlin-powered A Vs began to be displaced by A IIIs during August 1944, and both types were used in the Arnhem operation. A Vs lingered in service until the end of the war, and were even used during the Rhine crossing, (Operation *Varsity*) in March 1945.

39
Halifax B III (BS) PN381/D of No 1341 Flight, Digri, May 1945
No 1577 Flight had formed in 1943 to test the Halifax and Lancaster in India, operating mainly in the transport role. The second Halifax unit in the Far East was No 1341 Flight, which arrived in India in May 1945 for Elint operations, although as the war came to an end, the unit also performed transport duties. Painted in standard European Bomber Command camouflage, with dull red serials and codes, the flight's five aircraft had blue and white SEAC roundels and fin flashes. PN381 was unusual in having nose-art applied after its arrival in India. The No 1341 Flight aircraft had a similar antenna fit to the aircraft used by No 192 Sqn, but also had an additional DF loop antenna fairing below the rear fuselage. PN381 was SoC on 25 April 1946.

40
Halifax GR V Series I (Special) DG250/C of No 1674 Heavy Conversion Unit, Aldergrove, May 1945
No 1674 HCU was the training unit for aircrew destined for the meteorological reconnaissance squadrons, and it used a mix of types, including this almost unique Halifax. Unusual enough in combining the Z-type nose with rectangular tailfins, the aircraft also had the original Hudson-type mid-upper turret. It used Merlin 22 engines, driving four-bladed propellers, yet had Gallay radiators and the earlier lipped intakes. Despite its age and early features, the aircraft employed four-bladed propellers on all four engines. Having served tours with Nos 58 and 518 Sqns, DG250 had a very high demarcation line between the upper surface camouflage and the undersides. It also had a red individual aircraft code letter, which was perhaps a left-over from its service with No 58 Sqn, although that unit's OK- codes had been removed from this aircraft. This combat veteran was SoC on 20 July 1945.

FIGURE PLATES

1
Sgt A Stark, RAF, of No 466 Sqn, RAAF, at Driffield on 21 December 1943, is seen wearing his privately-purchased (or perhaps home-made) pullover. This has been donned over standard Battledress, with a Mae West laced over the top. He wears 1940 Pattern sheepskin flying boots, rather than the more common (by late 1943) 1941 Pattern, which added a leather ankle strap to prevent boot loss during parachute escapes. Stark also wears 1941 Pattern flying gauntlets, whose diagonal zip made them easier to don over a bulky Irvin jacket. Intended to be worn over silk or rayon liners, these thick, but supple, gloves were usually worn alone. Stark carries a C-type flying helmet, with distinctive triple press-stud fasteners for an E-type oxygen mask, to which is attached a pair of standard Mk VIII flying goggles, while the unattached mask is carried inside the helmet. Carrying helmets by the chin-strap was common practise, although it was officially discouraged.

2
Flt Sgt C Wilson, RAF, also of No 466 Sqn, RAAF, at Driffield on 21 December 1943. He is wearing the ubiquitous RAF Battledress blouse and trousers, which were initially issued specifically as flying clothing for use in the air only, over which more specialised garments were to be added. A Mae West is slung over the standard uniform Battledress, and a whistle is attached to the collar. Most aircrew customarily wore flying boots of one pattern or another, but some flew in ordinary uniform shoes. Wilson wears a normal NCO's uniform side hat, the Officers' Pattern of which was also favoured by some commissioned aircrew because it was easy to stow in a pocket or boot when exchanged for the usual flying helmet, and was less expensive than buying a second No 1 Uniform peaked cap. In colder weather, aircrew often added a thick pullover below the Battledress jacket, or substituted a sheepskin Irvin jacket, although these were bulky and heavy, and restricted movement.

3
Flt Lt R Kemp, RAF, of No 51 Sqn at Snaith on 7 December 1944 is seen after completing LV397's 100th sortie. He wears Mk VIII goggles pushed back on his C-Type leather flying helmet, from which hangs an H-type mask - a rarity among bomber aircrew, who tended to use the G-type mask. Finally, Kemp wears a Mae West and parachute harness over his RAF Battledress, and 1943 pattern escape boots. He carries a parachute pack in his right hand and a bag of maps and other equipment in his left.

4
Rear gunner from No 466 Sqn at Driffield on 21 January 1944. This anonymous individual, jubilant after a successful sortie, is fully kitted

out for the rigours of the Halifax rear turret. He wears an electrically-heated liner under a 1941 pattern Sidcot suit, over which he has donned the standard Mae West and separate parachute harness, rather than the combined parachute harness and life preserver favoured by many rear gunners. He has pushed his C-type flying helmet sideways off his head, and wears a B-type oxygen mask, with a shortened version of the straight non-articulated Mk III oxygen tube adaptor. Thick woollen stockings are turned back over the tops of his 1941 pattern fleece-lined brown suede flying boots. To this ensemble would be added electrically-heated gloves, socks and 'booties'.

5

Flt Lt Ron Hines, RAAF, of No 462 Sqn, RAAF, at Foulsham in 1945. As an 'Aussie', Hines wore Australian battledress, which was of a considerably darker hue than the equivalent RAF uniform. Underneath this, he wears a non-standard and non-uniform round-necked jumper over his service shirt and tie. Over this is his Mae West and then his parachute harness. He carries his seat-type parachute pack, which will be clipped to the harness before take-off. In his other hand, Hines carries his Type C leather flying helmet, G-type oxygen mask and gauntlet-type gloves. He wears 1943 pattern escape boots, designed to allow the zipped suede upper to be cut away, thus leaving the wearer with ordinary-looking laced leather walking shoes.

6

Mid-fuselage or 'Beam' gunner of No 35 Sqn at Linton-on-Ouse in March 1941. He is wearing the full winter flying rig used by Bomber Command in the early years of the war, including the Irvin thermally-insulated flying suit in thick pile sheepskin. The trousers were supported by built in braces, and featured separating zips running along each leg to allow easy removal for wound treatment. This is almost certainly the wired version of the suit, with connectors allowing the wearer to 'plug-in' electrically heated gloves and boot liners. He is also wearing 1939 pattern flying boots, with their distinctive vulcanised canvas tops. Despite this, the waterproofing was ineffective, and the boots often absorbed moisture and froze at high altitudes! On top of his bulky Irvin suit, this gunner wears an Irvin Harnessuit, which was a one-piece heavy cotton suit without arms or legs, incorporating a full webbing harness and life preserver bladder. This is one of three versions, incorporating clips for a parachute chest pack only. Another version had clips for a seat pack only, and a third had provision for either. Finally, the gunner wears a B-type flying helmet with its distinctive zippered earphone pockets, to which is attached the standard early-war Type D constant flow oxygen mask, with Type 19 microphone.

BIBLIOGRAPHY

MOYES, P J R, *The Handley Page Halifax B III, VI, VI.* Profile Publications, 1965

MOYES, P J R, *Handley Page Halifax Merlin-engined variants.* Aerodata

JONES, GEOFFREY, *Night Flight.* Kimber, 1981

SMITH, ARTHUR C., *Halifax Crew.* Carlton, 1983

BINGHAM, VICTOR, *Halifax - second to none.* Airlife, 1986

RAPIER, BRIAN J., *Halifax at War.* Ian Allan, 1987

ROBERTSON, BRUCE, *Halifax Special.* Ian Allan, 1990

MERRICK, K. A., *The Handley Page Halifax.* Aston, 1990

HMSO, *Bomber Command*

HMSO, *Bomber Command Continues.* 1942

HASTINGS, MAX, *Bomber Command.* Michael Joseph, 1979

TERRAINE, JOHN, *The Right of the Line.* Hodder, 1985

HARVEY, MAURICE, *The Allied Bomber War 1939-1945.* Spellmount, 1992

DELVE, KEN and JACOBS, PETER, *The Six Year Offensive.* Arms & Armour Press, 1992

FREEMAN, ROGER. A., *Raiding the Reich.* Arms & Armour Press, 1997

OVERY, RICHARD, *Bomber Command* 1939-1945. HarperCollins, 1997

BOWYER, CHAZ, *Bomber Barons.* Kimber, 1983

BOWYER, MICHAEL J. F., *Aircraft for the Many.* PSL, 1995

MOYES, PHILIP, *Bomber Squadrons of the RAF and their Aircraft.* MacDonald, 1964 and 1976

RAWLINGS, JOHN D. R., *Coastal, Support and Special Squadrons of the RAF and their Aircraft.* Jane's 1982

HALLEY, JAMES J., *The Squadrons of the Royal Air Force.* Air-Britain Publications

HALLEY, JAMES J., *Royal Air Force Aircraft Serials, various volumes.* Air-Britain Publications

JEFFORD C. G. Wg Cdr, *RAF Squadrons.* Airlife, 1988

DELVE, KEN, *The Source book of the RAF.* Airlife, 1994

STURTIVANT et al, *Royal Air Force Flying Training and Support Units.* Air Britain, 1998

BENNETT D. C. T. AVM, *Pathfinder.* Frederick Muller, 1958

STREETLY, MARTIN, *Confound and Destroy.* MacDonald and Janes, 1978

STREETLY, MARTIN, *Aircraft of No 100 Group.* Hale, 1984

BOWMAN, MARTIN AND CUSHING T., *Confounding the Reich.* PSL, 1996

BOWYER, CHAZ, *For Valour.* Grub St, 1992

TURNER JOHN FRAYN, *VCs of the Air.* Airlife, 1993

PRODGER, MICK J., *Luftwaffe vs RAF.* Schiffer, 1997

AEROSPACE PUBLISHING, Wings of Fame, Volume 8 'Halifax Variants'. 1998

BIDDLE, TAMI DAVIS, 'British and American Approaches to Strategic Bombing', published in *Air Power in Theory and Practise by John Gooch.* Cass, 1995

PARKS, W. HAYS, 'Precision and Area Bombing - who did which, and when?', published in *Air Power in Theory and Practise by John Gooch.* Cass, 1995